Spectatorship at the Elizabethan Court

Herausgegeben von
Susanne Scholz und Daniel Dornhofer

Vittorio Klostermann · Frankfurt am Main

Dieses Heft wurde mit einer DFG-Sachbeihilfe im Rahmen des Projekts *Den Hof machen. Zur Konstitution des höfischen Raums in England der Frühen Neuzeit* finanziert.

Inhalt

Susanne Scholz and Daniel Dornhofer

Introduction

Spectatorship and the Making of Early Modern Courtly Space

In sonnet 53 of Philip Sidney's *Astrophil and Stella*, Astrophil describes how he fares at a tournament in Stella's presence. When still hoping for her attention, he performs well, »Youth, luck and praise even filled my veins with pride« (l. 4). The concerted intervention of Cupid and Stella's gaze, however, undermine this hard-won self-confidence and he fails in the joust, blinded by her gaze, as it were: »I looked, and Stella spied, / Who hard by made a window send forth light. / My heart then quaked, then dazzled were mine eyes, / One hand forgot to rule, th'other to fight« (ll. 8-11).[1] The trope of the life-giving, but possibly also disempowering eye of the beloved, ingrained in the very constellation of the star lover and the star, and made familiar by droves of courtly literature, gives voice to one of the central concerns of Elizabethan court culture. To be seen by the queen, to be acknowledged as a player in the courtly arena, was tantamount to existing at all. The Elizabethan court, like that of any monarch reigning by personal rule, regulated status on the basis of spatial protocols prescribing degrees of distance or proximity to the queen's body. As a sequence of concentric or centripetal rooms around the innermost sanctum, the queen's bedchamber, the court can also be imagined as a series of thresholds to be crossed, every boundary marked by an official gate keeper who took care that it remained unviolated. From the Bouge of Court and the Book of Diet (which regulated who had a right to be fed and lodged at court) to the careful assignment of rooms, e. g. when on progress, the court was regulated by allotments of space and rights of access. The special case of a female, unmarried monarch accounted for an even greater concentration on the central person at court, the queen. It also created some structurally gendered spaces: the inner circle with the closest access to the queen consisted of the Ladies of the Bedchamber, creating a female space around the body natural of the queen, a female zone where symbolic and natural bodies met.[2]

1 Sir Philip Sidney, *A Critical Edition of the Major Works*, ed. Katherine Duncan-Jones, Oxford 1989, pp. 173-174.

2 On the structure of the Elizabethan court cf. Pam Wright, »A Change in Direction. The Ramifications of a Female Household, 1558 – 1603«, in: David Starkey et al., *The English Court: From the Wars of the Roses to the Civil War*, London, New York 1987, pp. 147-172.

1. Observing observers

When Elizabeth I., in her famous address to Parliament in 1586, claimed that princes were set on stages for all the world to observe, she also fashioned the court as a visual arrangement with the monarch at its centre. Scholarship of the last 30 years has pointed out that courtly life in the early modern period took place in a highly theatrical environment; that it was about performance, self-display, and successful engagement of the monarch's attention by making oneself into an object of (first of all) visual interest.

So unsurprisingly, in thinking about vision and the court, notions of spectatorship and observation are always close at hand. In courtly entertainments, but also in diplomatic correspondence and foreign travel narratives, the court emerges as a complex visual field in which images of the monarch, visual relations between sovereign and courtiers and the spatial arrangements in which these exchanges take place interact with each other. Every description of courtly interaction carries with it some hint of the awareness of being seen while walking, talking, parading one's clothes, dancing or fencing; there is always an element of the theatrical in the courtly self, a dimension of performing for an audience of spectators.[3]

The contributions to the conference on »Spectatorship and the Making of Early Modern Courtly Space«, from which this volume derives, focused on interactions of vision, identity and space, e. g. in dramatic performance at court, in entertainments on progresses, and in courtly dance. Courtly practices such as dancing, theatrical performance and spectacle, progresses, masques and, with an eye at the date of the conference, 17 November, accession day festivities – just like the literary representations of these activities – rely on visuality and the careful positioning of spectators and audiences, and by doing so generate and fashion courtly space. What all these instances of visual (self-)representation shared was the presence of a ›third figure‹, an external eye, as it were, that seemed to be written into the respective texts and that often appeared to have a special kind of agency in the cultural practices and courtly performances surrounding Elizabeth.

Reflecting on the court in terms of spectatorship spawns a number of concepts from visual culture studies that can be made productive in the analysis of courtly performance (and we are taking some of our cues from Janette Dillon's seminal

3 »Theatricality, in the sense of both disguise and histrionic self-presentation, arose from conditions common to almost all Renaissance courts: a group of men and women alienated from the customary roles and revolving uneasily around a center of power, a constant struggle for recognition and attention and a virtually fetishistic emphasis upon manner.« Stephen Greenblatt, *Renaissance Self-Fashioning. From More to Shakespeare*, Chicago 1980, p. 162.

The Language of Space in Court Performance)[4]: surveillance, observation, attention, witnessing, rapture, presence, and vibrancy, i. e. the effect or aura the royal body creates for those around the monarch. All of these involve forms of spectation, sometimes openly, sometimes clandestinely, or they describe the effects of an act of spectation on the courtier. Among these terms, surveillance is of course the practice in which the observing gaze is most strongly foregrounded.[5] In the light of modern techniques of surveillance, Elizabethan practices of obtaining visual information seem rather harmless, but knowledge or even rumours about their existence were enough to produce anxiety. Even if surveillance might be too harsh a term for the practice, a persistent, even violent gaze, if not exercised by the queen herself then at least in her service, creates a climate of permanent observation which can maybe be seen as an additional hypostasation of the interaction of social gazes that every member of the court (and to an even greater extent every outsider) was subject to, and made a subject by.

On the other side of the spectrum, rapture when being in the queen's presence, as it is described as a reaction of visual admiration or even adoration, e. g., during processions of Elizabeth, draws on the notion of a benign, even life-giving, gaze emanating from the queen. As in the case of surveillance, but with different effects, it ascribes almost supernatural power to the queen's gaze.

Obviously, then, describing the court as a visual constellation or a visual field prompts the question of actors and agency. Who looks at whom and which consequences do these interchanges of gazes have? How is the figure of an ›external eye‹ which is watching everybody's steps almost day and night dealt with? Courtly spectators monitored each other's performance in a highly competitive world, so seeing and being seen were among the central self-techniques at court, so much so that we could claim that the courtly subject emerges in the eye of the other, and, of course, the queen. Spectatorship, this is to say, was one of the formative agencies in courtly life. In this scopic constellation, peer-to-peer-gazing was only one side of the disciplinary ›coin‹. Even more important was the queen's gaze, because it provided status. So life at court was characterized by a complex regime of gazes, centring on the queen but by no means exercised by her alone, which positioned the individual courtier and negotiated his/her position at court.

4 Janette Dillon, *The Language of Space in Court Performance, 1400 – 1625*, Cambridge 2010.

5 Cf. John M. Archer, *Sovereignty and Intelligence. Spying and Court Culture in the English Renaissance,* Stanford 1993, esp. pp. 41-66.

2. Vision and the making of courtly space

If the court is a visual arrangement in which status emerges from the interaction of gazes, it is also a spatial arrangement demanding a specific proxemics, i. e. a hierarchy of spatial distance regulated by certain protocols. Whatever her movements were, the zone around the body of the queen was created by symbolic forms of deference (donning and doffing of hats, e. g.) and it overlapped with a ›zone of visibility‹ which also surrounded the queen and which it was the ambition of every courtier to enter.[6] The spatial and the visual ›axes‹ meet, for example, in the notion of attention, which is a courtly currency predicated on both spatial proximity and visual interest. Engaging the queen's attention can be seen as the ultimate aim of courtly performance, bringing the successful object of visual interest closer to the centre of power and enhancing his subject status in the process.

In courtly rhetoric, Elizabeth's gaze (the medium of her attention) was fashioned, in many performances and poetic representations, as the formative agent both of the courtly self and of the social order as a whole. Edmund Spenser's hyperbolic address to Elizabeth as »Great Lady of the greatest Isle, whose light / Like *Phoebus* lampe throughout the world doth shine«[7] is only one case in point. We have claimed before that the queen's gaze is charged with almost divine powers. This may be accounted for by the fact that Renaissance optics had different notions of how vision works, drawing on, among others, Platonic and Euclidian notions of sight.[8] Intromission theory claimed that rays emerge from the object in the visual field, and are then processed by the eye which thus makes meaning out of sensual perception (this is close to how optics today describes the working of human vision). Extramission theory, by contrast, maintained that the eye itself emits rays which bring the seen object into being. Originally advocated by Plato, extramission could be described as a (Platonic) »projection of internal archetypal patterns onto the world«[9], while intromission formed the basis for a ›nominalistic‹ way of making sense from the objects themselves. Whether it was

6 Frank Whigham, *Ambition and Privilege. The Social Tropes of Elizabethan Courtesy Theory*, Berkeley 1984, p. 47.

7 Edmund Spenser, *The Faerie Queene*, ed. A. C. Hamilton, London and New York 1987, I proem 4, ll. 3-4.

8 On Renaissance optics cf. John Shannon Hendrix and Charles H. Carman (eds.), *Renaissance Theories of Vision*, Farnham 2010; Robert S. Nelson (ed.), *Visuality Before and Beyond the Renaissance. Seeing as Others Saw*, Cambridge 2000; David Lindberg, *Theories of Vision from Al-Kindi to Kepler*, Chicago 1976.

9 Michael Camille, »Before the Gaze: the internal senses and late medieval practices of seeing«, in: Nelson (as note 8), pp. 197-223, here 206.

still valid as an optical theory or not, extramission theory provided a factual and metaphorical basis for a courtly rhetoric of vision in which the zone of visibility around the queen was conceptualized as a cone of rays emerging from her eyes which brought to life everything within the reach of the cone, but which left ›dead‹ whatever was outside.

Courtly spectators monitored each other's performance in a highly competitive world, where being seen by the monarch, that is, having her eyes light on him, virtually brought the courtier into being. On the other hand, the event of seeing the queen could also have an identity producing effect. Waiting, in expectant tension, for the monarch to appear, gazing at the spectacle of the royal body and sharing that experience of awed adoration with others could create a sense of joint elevation, thus bringing forth a community of spectators which, by gazing at her, acknowledged and confirmed her power and in a sense recharged her regal aura. Since this experience is frequently conveyed in literary representations, we could also speak of an imagined community of ›spectators‹ witnessing the queen in the knowledge that others share this reading experience: an imagined community in Benedict Anderson's sense.

Yet the burden of permanent observation not only troubled courtiers and ladies but also the monarch, who was bound to fulfil the visual expectations of her subjects, to look the part at all times. Being at the centre of a visually structured force field invests the central eye of that field with immense power, but it also demands a permanent effort with no escape from the gazes directed at her. However, the last years of Elizabeth's reign constituted a time of profound change, in which different, and often conflicting, perceptions of knowledge, of society, of the subject co-existed: With emerging notions of visual objectification on the horizon, making yourself into a spectacle could turn out to be an ambivalent experience.

The contributions to this volume show that spectatorship could have a whole variety of forms, functions and meanings. They investigate how Elizabethans at court (and sometimes outside it) negotiated the disturbing ambivalences of the royal gaze and the (in-)formative value of acts of spectation.

In the first contribution to this volume, Janette Dillon defines central categories for the analysis of spectatorship at the early modern court. Making use of insights from art historian Jonathan Crary, she stresses that spectatorship is not just about seeing, but essentially about complying with a system of conventions and limitations. Her source is the account of German nobleman Lupold von Wedel who witnessed the London Accession Day festivities in 1584. The traveler noted that the primary object of the day's tournament was not to win the prize but to amuse and impress the queen and the other spectators. The close examination of his account highlights the importance of three aspects of spectatorship: the nature of the space, the composition of the spectators, and the purpose and quality of the spectacle (where? who? and how and why?). While Elizabeth featured as prime spectator and prime performer in all courtly events, regimes of the gaze and protocols of space could be dramatically different. Dillon here examines the royal procession and the tournament as contrasting forms of spectacle that require different kinds of viewing, and are fraught with different kinds of both anxiety and pleasure.

Sasha Garwood's article explores Queen Elizabeth's careful and conscious manipulation of the performed language of food, starvation and the body and analyses its cultural implications. Eating at the Elizabethan court was fraught with symbolic meaning. As a ruler, Elizabeth used both elaborate ceremony and rare instances of shared or communal eating as political tools, implying intimacy or alliance accurately or otherwise. Both consumption and food refusal constituted public performances and were the subject of fierce speculation. Even amongst those habitually denied the queen's presence or sight of her person, changes in her body or eating habits were discussed avidly and reported internationally, scrutinized minutely for indications of intentions, feelings, responses or possible political moves. That during the crisis induced by Katherine Grey's pregnancy Elizabeth was ›falling away [...] extremely thin and the colour of a corpse‹ was reported to ambassador de la Quadra ›from three different sources‹ as well as ›a person who has the opportunity of being an eye witness‹. Accurately or otherwise, alteration in food intake is immediately interpreted by court audiences as a politically significant emotional expression.

Susanne Scholz' contribution provides insights into the politics of royal dancing. Especially Elizabeth's dances with the Earl of Leicester seem to loom large in the cultural imaginary of our time. Historical evidence of the queen's dances, however, is almost non-existent, while some poetical representations of the 1590s, John Davies' *Orchestra* as well as Book VI of Spenser's *The Faerie Queene*, seem to explicitly comment on the monarch's refusal to dance. Scholz argues that this is due to an increasing eroticization (through the spectators' gazes) of the dancing body concomitant with the emergence of couple dance as the dominant way of dancing in the early modern period. Gendering the queen's body, however, undermines its capacity of representing the body politic, resulting in Elizabeth's refusal to make use of dance as part of her royal self-representation.

Jackie Watson considers in her article the early modern Inns of Court as both a legal training ground and a ›finishing school‹ for gentlemen. As well as potential lawyers, many members had aspirations to work for the royal court. The growth of humanist education at the Inns and the universities during the sixteenth century enabled those of non-aristocratic background to find employment in the business of state conducted at home and abroad. The paper explores how the Inns, through the broad cultural education they provided, prepared young men to perform successfully at the royal court. It explores how participation in revels, which aped courtly hierarchies and procedures, highlight the nature of this preparation. The satirical and dramatic depictions of court life associated with the late Elizabethan Middle Temple are particularly revealing in order to establish the views of a notorious group of writers and wits, and their influential attitudes to courtly behaviour and appearance as the reign of Elizabeth drew to a close.

Simon Smith's article investigates the music of *Richard III* – exclusively trumpets and drums – which rarely receives the level of attention given to songs and music in other Elizabethan plays. The final four acts of *Richard III* each contain one royal entrance announced formally with a trumpet call, introducing the four monarchs represented in the play. Smith takes a close look at the instruments used on such occasions and the conventions that determined the spectators' expectations on hearing such calls and asks how an early modern audience would have understood and engaged with the playhouse sounds of the trumpet. He argues that to early modern ears, drum and trumpet calls had precise significations that were often integral to the narrative of dramatic performance. Thus, the sound of the trumpet would momentarily and imaginatively remake the playhouse as a courtly space, into which the royal figure would enter. But instead of offering an unequivocally glorious sight to revel in, the entries of the four different kings in *Richard III* directly challenge the expectations raised and keep drawing the audience's attention back to the question of what good kingship might look like. The article thus suggests that dramatically subtle use of playhouse music is not necessarily synonymous with extensive instrumental resources, or even with sophisticated music.

In the final article of this volume, Galena Hashhozheva considers the function of Hamlet's Mousetrap as a courtly prank. Shortly after its performance, Polonius insists that Hamlet's »pranks have been too broad to bear with.« »Pranks« is usually glossed as »wicked deeds«, yet the sense »practical jokes« – tricks that amuse by making fools of others – is also relevant in light of how much entertainment Hamlet derives from the play. The Mousetrap, she argues, can be fruitfully discussed in connection with Castiglione's theory of the practical joke. He deems »iestes and meerie pranckes« an indispensable part of courtly life, both because they provide amusement and because they can potentially have a moral-corrective function if the prankster knows the victim and his/her character. Pranks force victims to act out, usually in public, their moral flaws and may eventually have a therapeutic effect, and the Mousetrap participates in this Renaissance tradition. Hashhozheva shows how the Mousetrap both abides by and deviates from the Italian's prescriptions. Although Hamlet otherwise holds courtly manners in contempt, in the Mousetrap he avails himself of the custom of the courtly prank quite pragmatically and invests its moral-corrective matrix with his artistic sensibility, his epistemological obsessions, and a cold cruelty that marks a turning point in his course of action.

The different instances of spectatorship discussed in these case studies of different courtly events and environments not only testify to a great spectrum of visual practices at the Elizabethan court, they also articulate a consciousness, on the part of the actors on the social parquet of being at the same time subject and object of a gaze whose formative impact cannot be, and was not, underestimated. And since these practices have not ceased to be in operation, although the arenas of acknowledgement and recognition might have changed, we want, at the end of this introduction, to thank those who are our (not always visible) spectators in the courts of academic performance: Thanks are due to the German Research Association (DFG) whose funding has made both conference and publication possible and the Frankfurter Forschungszentrum für Historische Geisteswissenschaften for providing, literally, the space in which to perform. But thanks are also due to the audiences who commented on our performance and by their acts of critical spectation made this a better book.

Janette Dillon

Spectatorship at the Early Modern English Court

This paper seeks to analyse spectatorship at the early modern court; and because it started life at a conference in Germany on 17 November, the Accession Day of Elizabeth I, it focuses on a German visitor observing the English court in performance in 1584, in particular on his account of the Accession Day tournament at Whitehall on 17 November 1584. But first I wish to address the question of spectatorship more generally in order to establish a framework for analysis. The art historian Jonathan Crary has given extensive consideration to ways of seeing and constructing visual works of art at specific moments in history. Though his focus is primarily on nineteenth- and early twentieth-century visual art, some of his general statements are very suggestive for the study of spectatorship more widely and in earlier historical periods. »Problems of vision then, as now«, he writes, »were fundamentally questions about the body and the operation of social power«.[1] This is an observation as relevant to the analysis of sixteenth-century spectatorship as to later modes of seeing, and will shape the framework for analysis that I offer here.

Crary's quarrel with existing narratives of movements in the visual arts is that they routinely present such movements as the appearance of a new phenomenon to an observer who remains perceptually the same, or whose historical status is never interrogated.[2] But the history of art, he argues, effectively coincides with a history of perception. And perception exists only in relation to those who perceive. »Vision and its effects«, he writes, »are always inseparable from the possibilities of an observing subject who is both the historical product *and* the site of certain practices, techniques, institutions, and procedures of subjectification.«[3]

Crary rightly insists, then, that spectatorship is not just about seeing, which is why he prefers the word ›observer‹ to the word ›spectator‹, because its root does not mean ›to look at‹. It means ›to conform one's action, to comply with‹, as in the observation of rules, codes and established social practice. An observer, in other words, is »one who is embedded in a system of conventions and limitations«.[4]

1 Jonathan Crary, *Techniques of the Observer: On Vision and Modernity in the Nineteenth Century*, Cambridge, Mass., 1990, p. 3.

2 Ibid., p. 5.

3 Ibid., p. 5.

4 Ibid., pp. 5-6.

Bearing these emphases in mind, then, let us turn to look at Elizabeth's Accession Day tournament in 1584 through the eyes of a German observer called Lupold von Wedel; and let us begin by taking Crary seriously and building a picture of this observer in his own historical place and time. Von Wedel was a younger son of a noble German family, who left home at the age of about thirty to spend much of the next twenty years travelling. As Gottfried von Bülow, his nineteenth-century translator, notes: »he must have had good recommendations from and to very influential persons«, as he was able to travel freely, including a visit to Scotland.[5] Von Bülow further speculates that some political mission may have motivated his visit to England and Scotland, since he was met at the Scottish border by a group of gentlemen who escorted him as far as Dunbar, welcoming him in the King of Scotland's name. Von Wedel does not, however, report any meeting with either the King of Scotland or the Queen of England, or any of their Council, and his writing is in the form of a journal apparently kept for himself rather than a report to any political master, so the writing is not, so far as we can see, distorted by any obvious sense of mission or agenda. In addition, as von Bülow notes, von Wedel's writing is simple and straightforward, and unembellished to the point of awkwardness on occasion.

On the other hand, of course, von Wedel, merely because he is free of certain specifically English and court-based biases, is not a neutral observer. There can be no such thing. Like any and every observer, then as now, von Wedel is subject to the limitations and ideological biases of his own time and place. The things that seem to him notable or striking do so because he is positioned in particular ways. But because the things he notices are precisely *not* routinely the same things as might have struck an English observer as noteworthy, his observations can be very illuminating about both the spectacle itself and its particularly English qualities. Furthermore, where his observations coincide with English sources, they offer very useful endorsement of material that might otherwise seem dubious.

The first thing von Wedel tells us is the physical site occupied by the Queen and her ladies for the event. They placed themselves, he writes,

> at the windows in a long room at Weithol (Whitehall) palace, near Westminster, opposite the barrier (lists) where the tournament was to be held [ein lauk Zimmer, so jegen der Ban auf dem Hause Weithol bei Westmunster in die Finster gestellet] From this room a broad staircase led downwards . . . [zu dem Zimmer van der Bane eine breite Treppen gangen. . .].[6]

5 Gottfried von Bülow, »Journey Through England and Scotland Made by Lupold Von Wedel in the Years 1584 and 1585«, *Transactions of the Royal Historical Society*, New Series IX (1895), pp. 223-270, here p. 225.

6 Ibid., p. 258. References to Von Wedel's original German text are taken from *Lupold von Wedels Beschreibung seiner Reisen und Kriegserlebnisse: 1561 – 1606*, ed. Max Bär Stettin, Hessenland,

So there is a special viewing area defined by class and gender, specifically for the Queen and her ladies. Such separation of men from women was characteristic of the tournament, but not necessarily of other kinds of early modern ceremony. Where it *was* observed, however, it was normally an elite practice, and it is one that von Wedel comments on elsewhere in his observations of court occasions. He describes, for example, separate rooms of married and unmarried ladies dining apart from the men at the Lord Mayor's banquet.[7] And we see this noted elsewhere in descriptions of English court practice by other foreign visitors (see e. g. note 10 below).

This detail of the separate viewing area for the Queen and her ladies, and its prominence, as the first thing von Wedel notices, also provides very clear confirmation of Crary's general point that seeing is determined by the body and the »operation of social power«. What the Queen and her ladies see will be very different from what von Wedel sees, both physically and conceptually, because their viewing positions are so differently determined by their gender and their relative social positions. The Queen is situated at the apex of English court society, and her viewing is correspondingly powerful, privileged and free, in the sense that there is no-one above her with any right to impose controls. The Queen herself will of course have imposed her own voluntary and involuntary controls over what she saw. Though not a subject in the political sense, since she was monarch over her subjects, she was, like every human being, a subject in the wider, philosophical sense. As a perceiving self she was as specifically and socially determined as any of her subjects, though very differently so. As Queen, her rank overcame the limitations of her body. As a woman in sixteenth-century society, she would normally have been deemed inferior to men in most social situations; but as a Queen she not only rose to the top of the social pyramid, but also raised with her the ladies of her court into a position that, under a King, would have been occupied by men.

Von Wedel, though not one of Elizabeth's subjects, came from a sufficiently hierarchical society himself to defer unquestioningly to monarchical authority, whether male or female, and to document without question or surprise the careful privileging and enclosure of the Queen's spectating position. Outside the special viewing area for the Queen and her ladies, the genders mixed freely, including both married and unmarried women, as von Wedel notes: »file tausent Leute van Mannen, Weibern und Metlin«.[8] The careful distinction between married

1895, digitally reproduced by the University of Düsseldorf at http://digital.ub.uni-duesseldorf.de/ihd/content/structure/2250839. This quotation is from the ›Reise nach England‹, p. 353. The German sentences in the original are so long, however, that it is often impossible to match them up fully grammatically with the English quotations.

7 Von Bülow (as note 5), p. 254.

8 ›Reise nach England‹ (as note 6), p. 353.

and unmarried women in this otherwise neutral phrase suggests some difference between English and German practice in terms of freedom for women; and indeed von Wedel has already registered surprise at the relative prominence and freedom of female spectators below the rank of the Queen and her ladies elsewhere in his account of his travels. He notes, for example, on the occasion of the installation of the Lord Mayor of London, that the crowd inside the Guildhall was of »men as well as women, for the English women want to be present on all such occasions [nicht alleine van Mannen sundern auch Weibern, wie dan die engelschen Weiber bei allen Sachen sein wullen]«.[9] Again, the relative freedom of English women is a phenomenon endorsed by other foreign observers.[10]

Absence of gender regulation, then, clearly struck von Wedel quite forcefully; but more striking to an English spectator, and particularly distinctive of the tournament as a form of court spectacle, was its openness in class terms, which von Wedel again reports without comment: »ein jeder welcher zusen wult und einen Stant haben, musste 18 [sic] Pfenning geben«.[11] Anyone who could pay the entry fee of twelve English pennies, then (the figure of twelve is from von Bülow's translation), could get a stand and see the performance; and thousands did. On the other hand, 12d was not cheap, and was a price that would exclude most ordinary working people. Entry to the public theatre at this time, by contrast, cost between 1d and 3d; and even fifteen years later the elite indoor playhouses were charging only 6d, half the cost of entry to a royal tournament in 1584. Even so, the very fact that access is not by invitation only distinguishes the tournament from most other forms of courtly entertainment. Again, as Crary insists, viewing, and what can be viewed, are determined by the operations of social power. The Queen and her court decide to make tournaments a form of display open to, and designed partly to impress, the wider public. Court masque, by contrast, and most forms of indoor entertainment, largely restricted entry to an invited elite, though there is some evidence of what Hall's Chronicle calls »the rude people« behaving roughly at such entertainments.[12] Hall occasionally

9 Von Bülow (as note 5), p. 254; ›Reise nach England‹ (as note 6), p. 348.

10 Tim Stretton quotes a Dutchman and another German on the freedom of English women as compared with those in other European countries. See »Women, Property and Law«, in: *A Companion to Early Modern Women's Writing*, ed. Anita Pacheco, Oxford: Blackwell, 2002, pp. 40-57, here p. 40.

11 ›Reise nach England‹ (as note 6), p. 353.

12 As Hall reports this occasion: » . . . soda[in]ly the rude people ranne to the pagent, and rent, tare, and spoyled the pagent, so that the Lord Stuard nor the head officers could not cause them to abstaine, excepte they shoulde have foughten and drawen bloud, and so was this pagent broken.
After the kyng and his compaignions had daunced, he apointed the ladies, gentelwomen and the Ambassadours to take the letters of their garmentes, in token of liberalitie, whiche thing the common people perceyvyng, ranne to the kyng, and striped hym into his hosen and dou-

reports them tearing at costumes or breaking up pageant wagons, and the Great Chronicle reports that Henry VIII actually gave instructions as to where this part of the intended audience should stand in order to assault the performers, including himself.[13]

Von Wedel goes on to describe the tournament itself, which exudes wealth, costing the combatants, by his estimate, »several thousand pounds each [es hat ime etzlige tausent Kronen gekostet]«.[14] Again, though von Wedel merely states what strikes him without making explicit personal comment, the implication is that he is impressed by the amounts spent; and this indeed would be the effect the participants were trying to achieve. In spending vast amounts of money on their pageants and costumes they were seeking to impress first the Queen, and secondly the other spectators, with their magnificence, their possession of sufficient wealth to display excess with ease. Theirs is a display of what Thorstein Veblen calls ›conspicuous consumption‹ – the deployment of excessive spending to display social superiority.[15] Again, then, what is on view is determined by the body and the operation of social power. The bodies of the combatants display their wealth and prowess; and the better and more accomplished the body, the more attractive and impressive the display. Further, what the body wears and bears, the armour, costumes, weaponry and so on, is determined by wealth – so again, the bigger the better, in the sense that the more elaborate and expensive the attire and accoutrements, the more eye-catching and memorable the spectacle is to the spectators. As the details of von Wedel's description confirm, immense care goes into preparing and presenting every aspect of each combatant's display, from the visual finery of the self to skill in horsemanship, musical accompaniment and the attire of servants, horses and chariots. Each combatant, furthermore, presents the Queen with »a costly present« [ein statliche Vorerung], which further emphasises the degree to which wealth determines the display and hence to some

blet, and all his compaignions in likewyse. Sir Thomas Knevet stode on a stage, and for all his defence he lost his apparell. The ladies likewyse were spoyled, wherfore the kynges garde came sodenly, and put the people backe, or els as it was supposed more inconvenience had ensued. So the kyng with the Quene and the ladyes returned into his chamber, where they had a great banket, and all these hurtes were turned to laughyng and game, and thought that, all that was taken away was but for honoure, and larges: and so this triumphe ended with myrth and gladnes«. Janette Dillon, *Performance and Spectacle in Hall's Chronicle*, London, 2002, p. 41.

13 According to the Great Chronicle, the King instructed his gentlemen ushers to set the Ambassadors' servants »at a certayn place where he shuld passe by, when the dysguysyng was endyd, and that they shuld not ffere to pull and tere the said Garment ffrom his body«. Cited in Dillon (as note 12), p. 192.

14 Von Bülow (as note 5), p. 259; ›Reise nach England‹ (as note 6), p. 354.

15 Thorstein Veblen, *The Theory of the Leisure Class: An Economic Study of Institutions*, London 1899, rpt 1924, passim. Veblen is talking about the nouveau riche of the nineteenth century; but the point is equally applicable to the Elizabethan aristocracy.

extent the outcome of the tournament.[16] For the main ›outcome‹ is not necessarily who wins on points, but who draws the most positive approval from the Queen.

Despite this heavy investment in the trappings of the event, however, it is not entirely serious, and this aspect of the event strikes von Wedel quite forcibly, again perhaps as unusual in his experience, though he does not say so:

> Some of the servants were disguised like savages [wilde Leute], or like Irishmen, with the hair hanging down to the girdle like women, others had horse manes on their heads, some came driving in a carriage, the horses being equipped like elephants, some carriages were drawn by men, others appeared to move by themselves; altogether the carriages were of very odd appearance.
>
> [. . . ire Gesinde zugericht wie wilde Leute, etzlige wie irlendische Leute mit langen Haren bis in den Gurtel wie die Weiber, etzlige halbe Mene auf den Kopfen gehabt, etzlige sein auf die Bane farende kummen, ir Pferde wie Elepfanten zugerichtt, etzlige sein faren kummen, welche Leute, so seltzem angethan, die Wagen gezogen, die anderen faren kummen, welche Wagen zugerichtt, dass sie silbest ane einiges Trecken gangen, wie den alle Wagen seltzem und sunderlich, doch etzliche zugerichtt wesen . . .] [17]

Even the face-to-face encounters with the Queen sometimes sought to amuse her:

> When a gentleman with his servants approached the barrier, on horseback or in a carriage, he stopped at the foot of the staircase leading to the queen's room, while one of his servants in pompous attire of a special pattern mounted the steps and addressed the queen in well-composed verses or with a ludicrous speech, making her and her ladies laugh.
>
> [Wan nun einer mit seiner Dienern auf die Bane kummen, ist er geritten oder gefaren bis an die Stigen, so an das Zimmer, da die Kuningin standen, gangen, so ist dan einer van seinen Dieneren die Stigen zu der Kuningin aufgangen, welcher gar wol geputzt und angetan, doch ein jeder sein egen Muster gehabt, lange zu der Kuningin als reimenweis, daruf ein jeder studieret, gerett und unterweisen seltzame Pussen kurzweilig doch zirlich und hublich an Tag geben, dass ofte die Kuningin nicht alleine sundern der Umstant lachen mussen wan er dan seine Rede fullendet . . .] [18]

When von Wedel describes a tournament three weeks later, set up in the same location and using the same barrier and benches as the Accession Day tournament, he makes the point that though it lacked the »pomp« [Pracht] of the earlier tournament, it was »more in earnest, for each party was bent to win the

16 Von Bülow (as note 5), p. 259; ›Reise nach England‹ (as note 6), p. 354.
17 Von Bülow (as note 5), p. 258; ›Reise nach England‹ (as note 6), pp. 353-354.
18 Von Bülow (as note 5), p. 259; ›Reise nach England‹ (as note 6), p. 354.

prize [file harter und ernesthaftiger, den ein jeder Del den Prisz gerne het haben mugen].«[19] In other words, the primary object of the Accession Day tournament was not to win the prize but to amuse and impress the Queen and the other spectators. ›Sprezzatura›, more than chivalric prowess, was what was primarily on display, and courtly spectators would have understood this.

Von Wedel's account thus alerts us to the importance of three aspects of spectatorship. First, we must attend to the nature of the space and the way it is laid out for performance. Here we know that the performance space (i. e. the barrier along and across which the combatants will fight) is enclosed by the seating stands and that there is a further, more enclosed and restricted space from which the Queen and the other elite female spectators view. This layout also shows us how gender and class are encoded into the space and the viewing conditions. The availability of entry to all by ticket demonstrates a kind of openness to the public, whilst the cost of entry shows how that openness is in fact restricted in practice.

Second, we must determine who constitute the spectators. From the space it is obvious that the nature and rank of the spectators determine their access and response to the spectacle. This is clear, first, from the way this spectacle addresses itself specifically to the Queen, with combatants' servants making speeches directly to her and offering presents to her in the name of their lords; and it is the Queen herself who then awards the prizes at the end of the tournament. But von Wedel himself is of course also a spectator, who notes on another occasion and in another venue (namely at the Whitehall preaching place) the special provision sometimes made by the Queen for foreign visitors, and not just those of ambassadorial rank. There is in that location, he writes:

> a high and spacious house with many windows and inside full of seats and benches one above the other, so that many people may be seated there. The ceiling is hung with leaves and thick bushes. When foreign gentlemen are present, the queen orders all sorts of amusements to be arranged here, while above in the bushes birds sing beautifully.
>
> [ein hoges und rumes Haus gefuret, welches merendel ful lauter Finster, sulchens ist inwendik ful Benken oder Sessel gemacht, einen uber dem anderen, da file Leute sitzen kunnen, und oben an dem Bodem ist es mit lauterem Lop und dicken Buschen beheuket.][20]

Clearly on some court occasions, then, foreign visitors were especially well accommodated and attended to. So who the spectators were was crucial to what they saw and how they judged and responded to it.

19 Von Bülow (as note 5), p. 262; ›Reise nach England‹ (as note 6), p. 358.
20 Von Bülow (as note 5), p. 236; ›Reise nach England‹ (as note 6), p. 324.

Thirdly, we must consider the purpose and quality of the spectacle and how it interpellates the spectators. Here it is evident that conspicuous wealth is a central part of the intended effect of the tournament and that it seeks to make a powerful impression on spectators at all levels of society. The courtiers taking part in the tournament compete to make themselves and their attendants visually striking. The English, in von Wedel's opinion, »are very rich and are fond of pomp and splendour [rich, vormugen, van groszer Pracht und Wollust]«.[21] At the same time it is important to note that high cost does not necessarily denote high seriousness. Some of the cost goes into prioritising outrageous and eccentric effects, and making the Queen laugh is evidently something of a priority on this occasion.

We might classify these categories more broadly as where? who? and how and why? I am not going to spend much time here discussing the ›where‹ of spectatorship, as that is a question that I have already discussed at length elsewhere.[22] Instead I want to look more closely at the interaction between who spectates and how and why the spectacle is staged, in order to describe more closely particular kinds of viewing.

Who?

As Susanne Scholz and Daniel Dornhofer suggest in the introduction to this volume, both the Queen and her courtiers have a high investment in viewing each others' performances: »While courtly spectators monitored each other's performance in a highly competitive world, Elizabeth's gaze was fashioned, in many performances and poetic representations, as the formative agent both of the courtly self and of the social order as a whole.« We can see from this Accession Day tournament, as with so many performances at the early modern court, that performance and spectatorship are not always separable, but intimately wrapped up together. Elizabeth is simultaneously chief spectator and chief performer. Even were she to sit unmoving in her seat throughout, she would still be a performer, since her very presence continually draws the eyes of all spectators; but of course she does not sit still. She participates by responding to speeches, accepting presents and awarding prizes. Her smiles or her laughter are in themselves a prize the combatants seek more eagerly in this kind of show-tournament than the prizes for military prowess. Their performance on this occasion is all about attracting and holding her gaze and becoming visible or remarkable in her eyes.

21 Von Bülow (as note 5), p. 262; ›Reise nach England‹ (as note 6), p. 358.

22 See further Janette Dillon, *The Language of Space in Court Performance 1400 – 1625*, Cambridge, 2010.

So the Queen and the combatants are participant-spectators, and the majority of the remaining spectators are made up of her ladies, who sit with her, and her non-participating courtiers, who watch jealously as others usurp the Queen's gaze and climb the ladder of favour in her eyes. Von Wedel goes into very little detail about the spectators on this occasion, other than simply to report the presence of many thousand spectators, of all genders, and including »citizens [Burgern]« as well as gentlemen and noblemen.[23] He does, however, report the behaviour of ordinary citizens at other appearances of the Queen, on her procession to and from chapel at Hampton Court, for example, and on her entry into London to visit St James's Palace, a few days before the Accession Day tournament. On both occasions the general formula is the same: reverence and awe from the people received with graciousness and a performance of humility from the Queen. The people fall to their knees in her presence and she responds with kindness and modesty. Describing her entry into London, von Wedel makes this point with particular emphasis:

> She sat alone by herself in the carriage, being clad in a white robe, and addressed the multitude saying, »Gott seve mi pippel« which is in German »Gott behüte Euch, mein Volck,« the latter answering, »Gott seve her grass« – in German »Gott behüte Euer Genade.« The people said this very often, falling on their knees.
>
> [In dem Wagen ist sie alleine geseszen in weisz gekleitt, zu dem Folke hat sie gesprochen »Got seve mi pippel« ist auf teutsch Gott behute euch mein Folk. Daruf das Folk geantwortet »Gott seve hor grasz«, auf teutsch: Gott behute euwer Genade. Sulchens sie ofte geschrigen und auf die Kne gefallen.][24]

This is interesting because it echoes other reports of popular behaviour, notably Mulcaster's account of Elizabeth's coronation entry, which has been criticised both because Mulcaster may not actually have been present in person and because of its propagandist agenda. But von Wedel's account of this same behaviour lends credence to the probability that this was how Elizabeth and her people actually did behave when they encountered each other.

The graciousness and courtesy of these exchanges, however, took place within a context of great excitement and some unruliness on the streets. »Crowds of people«, says von Wedel, »came running after – men, women, and young girls [nicht alleine Menner sundern Weiber und Junkfrowen]« and »[a]ll the time the procession lasted the bells were rung [man hat aber wie sie eingezogen, mit allen Klocken geleutet]«, so the emotional temperature was consciously being

23 Von Bülow (as note 5), p. 259; ›Reise nach England‹ (as note 6), p. 354.
24 Von Bülow (as note 5), p. 256; ›Reise nach England‹ (as note 6), p. 351.

whipped up by those organising the procession.[25] One further detail von Wedel supplies in relation to a different event, the installation of the Lord Mayor of London, gives us some indication of how packed and pressured such an eagerly spectating crowd might become. At the head of that procession, he reports, »there are some fire-engines ornamented with garlands, out of which they throw water on the crowd, forcing it to give way, for the streets are quite filled with people [forne her aber etzlige mit Spruszen gangen, so mit Lobe wol zugerichtt, damit die Feur gesprutzet, damit das Folk, weil die Gaszen ganz mit Folk bedrenget, weichen muste]«.[26]

How any of this behaviour might overlap with crowd behaviour at a tournament is open to speculation, but three things are clear:

First, tournament spectators are seated. There is no mention of standing spectators, and von Wedel's description indicates that the payment of 12d buys a seat. The performance and viewing space is enclosed and almost certainly policed by the Queen's guards. It is thus far less likely that there will be any significant unruliness or unrestrained behaviour than in a street procession.

Secondly, the distinct ownership of the two spaces differentiates the way spectators feel and respond. Whereas the tournament takes place in the environment of the court, inviting the spectators into the Queen's own space, and ranking and segregating its locales accordingly, the procession takes the monarch and the court into publicly owned space, into the streets where the spectators enact their daily business. The ›invitation‹, if we may call it such, is from the city and the people to the court rather than the other way round.

Thirdly, what emerges from the account of behaviour at processions is that the Queen is a supremely desirable object of attention; and the fascination of her person is as likely to structure the attention of spectators at a tournament as the attention of a crowd at a procession. It will structure the gaze of any public appearance she makes. Thus, though the combats have their own excitement, drawing the gaze to them especially at moments of high drama, the spectators' attention is also frequently and intensely focused on the Queen, for some spectators as much as on the spectacle of combat.

There is a crucial difference, however, between the nature of these two events and the way they interpellate their spectators, and I want to spend the remainder of this paper looking at the question of how particular kinds of spectatorship are called into being by the nature and purpose of different forms of spectacle.

25 Von Bülow (as note 5), pp. 256-257; ›Reise nach England‹ (as note 6), pp. 350-351.
26 Von Bülow (as note 5), p. 255; ›Reise nach England‹ (as note 6), pp. 348-349.

How and why?

We may begin by thinking further about the royal procession and the tournament as contrasting forms of spectacle, requiring different kinds of viewing. The royal procession, unlike the tournament or most other forms of court spectacle, is accessible to all classes of spectator at no cost. Its aim, in fact, is partly, even primarily, to reach those spectators who have no direct access to the court. It takes the court to them; seeks to make the monarch visible to the people in a form that appears attractive, gracious, humble and commands devotion; and it further seeks to impress the people with the splendour and beauty of the whole court. It seeks to inspire in them a sense that this entity of the court, including and representing the monarch, the ruling class and the country, is one in which they can take pride, one which has the right to demand their obedience and reverence and one whose dominance is thus accepted. Thus the situation von Wedel describes, in which the Queen, set apart in splendid isolation, issues quasi-loving pronouncements (»God save my people«) and the people respond to that seeming love with equal or greater affection (»God save her grace«) and with willing subjection (falling to their knees) is exactly what the procession, as event, seeks to produce.

The tournament, however, as a more exclusive event, occupying elite space, is aimed more at fellow courtiers than at the common people, and ranks its spectators, probably even more so than Von Wedel describes. A Venetian Ambassador describing seating arrangements for revels in 1527 at the court of Henry VIII, for example, reports three tiers of seats along the long sides of the hall, with men on the right and women on the left, the first for ambassadors, the second for noblemen and the third for »those to whom admission was granted, they being few«.[27] Almost certainly some similar ranking of seating was in place for tournaments admitting the wide range of spectators that these Accession Day tournaments did.

The Queen was both participant and spectator at this event, which meant that for all other spectators there was a markedly divided gaze. It is true of any event, early modern or otherwise, of course, that the gaze of spectators will wander to some extent, and will take in other spectators and the whole performance space as well as whatever is currently at the centre of the performance, asking to be viewed. But the Queen is an exceptional object of attention and will repeatedly draw the eyes of spectators away from the apparent centrepiece at the barrier, however colourful, varied and visually rich that centrepiece may be. (At the London Olympics the cameras kept returning to the Queen, sometimes embarrassingly for viewers at home, as the Queen was often to be seen looking bored or play-

27 Dillon (as note 12), p. 245.

ing with her fingers, while the commentators pretended to see evidence of her fascinated engagement with the spectacle.) For spectators at this kind of event, then, there is an ongoing push-pull between two central objects of attention, as well as all the peripheral elements. They must continually choose where to look in a show of competing centres, the one authoritative, still and self-contained (the Queen in her viewing chamber), the other full of movement, energy and excitement (the tournament).

By contrast, von Wedel's description of the procession into London, with the Queen sitting in lonely splendour in her carriage and people running after her, falling to their knees when they come alongside her and repeatedly addressing her with formulaic speeches of adoration, conveys the sense that, whatever the richness and diversity of the rest of the procession, the presence of the Queen as framed and moving centrepiece creates an ineluctable drive on the part of spectators to pursue that single object of attention with frenetic and uncontrolled energy. The two spectacles, then, create different kinds of viewing, fraught with different kinds of anxiety as well as pleasure. The plenitude of the tournament, with so many objects, sights and sounds continuously on view and demanding attention in an enclosed space, bombards and perhaps overwhelms the spectators, forcing them to choose where to direct their gaze and unsettling them with the endless flickering back and forth of choice. The moving spectacle of the procession, however, with each of its objects so briefly on view to the crowd it passes through, creates a different rhythm altogether. In place of the packing of multiple aesthetic stimuli into an enclosed and unchanging space over a period of hours, the procession offers a long rise of anticipation and of aesthetic objects of view experienced as preparatory to the climactic few moments of visual encounter with the central object of desire, followed by the slow falling away from that through gradually diminishing levels of spectacle.

Important too is the different placing of each of these spectacles on what might be called the register of play. The tournament is built around competitive play. The combats themselves are a kind of game. There is also a further layer of play in the fact that chivalry itself has become a nostalgic form of dressing up and playing at knighthood by the time of Elizabeth's reign. The further fact that on this occasion the knights dress their attendants in joky or eccentric ways, as Irishmen or savages, equip their horses to look like elephants and enter in odd-looking carriages that move in unpredictable ways suggests that there is a fundamental sense of comedy underlying the way this particular tournament functions.

Despite the prominence of comic play, however, the tournament has a strongly serious side which makes spectating, especially for courtier-spectators, heavily invested. (And we must remember that spectating is always different for each spectator, inflected by how each is positioned, socially and physically, and how each is interpellated by the event.) In contrast to the fictive context created by the costumes and probably the speeches, the competition between the combatants vying for the attention of the Queen is real and present. The fictional framework and humorous grotesquerie is a courteous embellishment masking the highly serious play that underlies the courtly game.

The procession, on the other hand, has no fictive element. It is entirely present in the moment. It is not only real but hyperreal, demanding and producing a heightened intensity of gaze that roots it so firmly in the moment that the surrounding reality of the city and everyday life seems somehow suspended while the spectators run after the procession, strive to come close to it and, if they are lucky enough to come close to the Queen, fall on their knees in recognition of the overwhelming sensation of such a moment. This is the kind of viewing that I have elsewhere already cited Jonathan Crary to explicate. In his words, it is a

> state of being suspended, a looking or listening so rapt that it is an exemption from ordinary conditions, that it becomes a suspended temporality, a hovering out of time. The roots of the word attention in fact resonate with a sense of ›tension‹, of being ›stretched‹, and also of ›waiting‹. It implies the possibility of a fixation, of holding something in wonder and contemplation, in which the attentive subject is both immobile and ungrounded.[28]

Crary returns us to the point where we began: that perception involves »more than the single-sense modality of sight«.[29] The word ›spectator‹, linked as it is, through etymology, to sight, is inadequate to represent the nature of the engagement a subject makes with a spectacle (again a term that privileges sight). Perceiving a procession, as von Wedel's account richly demonstrates, involves hearing, speech and motion, as well as deep roots in the order of power: subjects run, call out, fall to their knees and utter reverential good wishes against the perpetual sound of bells ringing, others shouting and the continuous press of bodies against bodies. Their spectatorship involves their whole being as it is at this moment in time.

28 Jonathan Crary, *Suspensions of Perception: Attention, Spectacle, and Modern Culture*, Cambridge, Mass. and London: MIT Press, 2001, p. 10; cited in Dillon (as note 22), p. 15.
29 Ibid., p. 3.

Sasha Garwood

Watching Elizabeth Eating

Power and the Politics of Penetration

Ritual and the rhetoric of royalty

The spectacle of eating at the Elizabethan court was fraught with symbolic meaning. As a ruler, Elizabeth used both elaborate and ultimately abstract ceremonies and rare instances of shared or communal eating as political tools. To be seen or reported sharing meals with the Queen connoted intimate access, implying alliance even when this may not necessarily have been the case. Elizabeth was capable of eating in public on occasion, as witness the spectacular nine-hour banqueting marathon following her coronation. However, even then not only was the guest list limited to the aristocracy (powerful in their own right) but even Il Schifanoya, the spectacularly gossipy Venetian ambassador (he for whom »banquets«, with their dangerous indulgence, constituted »levities and unusual licentiousness«), makes no mention of her actually eating, simply of her »drinking the healths« of »all« her noble servitors.[1] It is clear that the Queen quite consciously used actual shared consumption, as she did almost everything else, as a negotiating tactic – when she invited the same ambassador to eat in her Privy Chamber and discuss marriage negotiations, for example, he perceived it as an honour and was clearly disarmed by the prospect. Baron Caspar von Breuner, Imperial ambassador, describes a similar experience:

> She then invited me to breakfast with her, and after the meal spoke much and gaily and desired me to come on the river again in the evening. When I arrived there she invited me into her boat, made me take the helm and was altogether very talkative and merry. Everybody kept saying that such honour had never been shown to anyone but me.[2]

1 Rawdon Brown, G. Cavendish Bentinck (eds.), *Calendar of State Papers Relating to English Affairs in the Archives of Venice* (hereafter *CSP Venetian*), Vol 7, 1558 – 1580, London: Public Record Office, 1890, 11, see also App.2; 18.

2 Baron Caspar von Breuner to the Emperor Ferdinand, 13 June 1559, in: Victor von Klarwill (ed.), *Queen Elizabeth and Some Foreigners, being a series of hitherto unpublished letters from the archives of the Hapsburg family*, London 1928, p. 96. After three meetings with the Queen: For citation and discussion, see Ilona Bell, »Elizabeth I – Always Her Own Free Woman«, in: Carole Levin

The political spin involved – Breuner trying to convince his sceptical employers of his mission's success – in no way mitigates the »honour« both Breuner and others perceive in breakfasting with Elizabeth, or the very public nature of such gestures. To be seen eating with the Queen was evidently a great accolade.

Accordingly, like her fellow monarchs, she appears to have maintained occasional banquets as a fundamental means of honouring and negotiating with foreign nationals.[3] Il Schifanoya describes Elizabeth's lavish treatment of the French:

> They ... dined and supped with the Queen, not in the garden, but in the large wing (ala) of the palace, and being seen to do so publically [sic], they were honoured by everybody.[4]

She evidently sought to impress with the lavish hospitality of her royal office if not the extent of her personal consumption: the »utmost display« as Venetian Giacomo Soranzo put it.[5] Eating could be sex, power, assimilation: but the Virgin Queen approached matters very differently from her father's spectacularly staged consumption. Unlike Henry VIII's vast formal dinners, so memorably if apocryphally caricatured by Charles Laughton, for all the continued importance of formal dining ritual the Queen herself hardly ever ate in public.[6] Lupold von Wedel's account of his visit to England excitedly recounts a Christmastide meal, where the Queen sat alone at a public table: excitedly, because »at no other time throughout the whole year does the Queen dine in public«, and »only on feast days can a stranger see her at meals.«[7] Thomas Platter's 1599 *Travels in England* contains a detailed description of the Queen's elaborate »luncheon« ceremony, which is worth quoting in full to indicate the elaborate ritual involved in presenting the Queen's mealtimes:

> They bade us wait [...] in the audience chamber so as to see the Queen's luncheon being served; indeed every honour was shown us [...] when the Queen had returned to her chamber, her guardsmen [...] carried two tables into the

and Patricia A. Sullivan (eds.), *Political Rhetoric, Power, and Renaissance Women*, Albany, NY, 1995; or Alison Weir, *Elizabeth the Queen*, London: Pimlico 1998, p. 74.

3 Mentions of lavish banquets in the *CSP Foreign* definitely tail off, although this may have been because they became customary and assumed as standard. Interestingly, the English ambassador signalled his displeasure at the French court by refusing to attend a banquet; they were obviously a significant negotiating tool. See J. M. Rigg, *Calendar of State Papers Relating to English Affairs in the Vatican Archives* (hereafter *CSP Rome*), Vol 1, 1558 – 1571, p. 737; *CSP Venetian*, 1558 – 1580, App. 2.

4 May 30th, *CSP Venetian*, 1558 – 1580, p. 79. See also p. 76, 77, 126, App. 2.

5 E. g., *CSP Venetian*, 1558 – 1580, p. 77, App. 2.

6 *The Private Life of Henry VIII* (Alexander Korda, 1933), with its notorious image of Henry at a laden table throwing bones over his shoulder for the dogs.

7 von Klarwill (as note 2), p. 336.

> room with trestles, and set them down where the Queen had been sitting. Then another two entered, each bearing a mace and bowed three times; first at their entrance, and by the door, then in the centre of the room and lastly in front of the table, and after they had laid it down they withdrew again. Soon more guards in tabards appeared bowing with plates and other things which they laid on the table, and after they had laid it they withdrew again. Following them came another two bowing, and placed the carving knives, bread and salt on the table. Then a gentleman bearing a mace entered, together with a charming gentlewoman or lady-in-waiting, who bowed very gracefully as described above, thrice to the empty table, at the same time a gentleman with a mace arrived with another gentleman and all four stood before the table.
> Then straightaway came the Queen's guardsmen with red tabards folded back, one behind the other, and if I am not mistaken, a weapon at their sides, each one bearing a single covered dish of food. They are all very tall, fine, strong men, and all similarly attired, so that I never in my life saw their like. I believe there must have been forty of them.
> When they handed over the food a gentleman removed the cover, while the lady in waiting served and carved a large piece off, which she gave to the guard who had carried it in, and who was supposed to eat the portion, though they generally took it out or merely tasted a morsel.
> Two of them brought wine and beer which was also poured out and tasted. And after this long table had been fully laid and served and *the same obeisance (?) and honours performed as if the Queen herself had sat there*, whatever dishes there were, were offered to the Queen. in her apartment for her to make her choice. These were sent into her and she ate of what she fancied, *privily however, for she very seldom partakes before strangers*, and the remainder was carried out again to the lords' table; and the guards brought other fresh dishes, which were served like the former, and I observed among them some very large joints of beef, and all kinds of game, pasties and tarts. After the third course had been thus brought in, served, and removed again, and the dessert prepared and cleared off, the Queen's musicians appeared in the presence chamber with their trumpets and shawms, and after they had performed their music, everyone withdrew, bowing themselves out just as they had come in, and the tables were carried away ...[8]

»... *she very seldom partakes before strangers*, ...«[9] For a monarch so continuously manipulative of her own iconography, this is undoubtedly significant: offering a

8 Thomas Platter, *Thomas Platter's Travels in England 1599*, ed. Clare Williams, London: Jonathan Cape, 1937, pp. 193-195; emphases mine.
9 Ibid.; emphases mine.

public display of authoritative power, self-evident control over her own food intake, and resistance to both the implied possession by her public and the potential indignities of public consumption. Whilst Platter's account dates from the end of Elizabeth's reign, he gives no indication that the monarch's literal absence or this amount of ceremonial was a recent innovation. It is perhaps worth considering that even an account this detailed and extended is only concerned with the business of service. Perhaps unsurprisingly, Platter makes no mention of the vast efforts that were involved in preparation and presentation of the food; not only its assembly but its receptacles, coverings, cutlery and so on, in the kitchens and en route to the ceremonial chamber. The actual process of feeding the queen must have been in practical terms considerably more complex than even its elaborate ceremonial would indicate: J. L McIntosh's *From Heads of Household to Heads of State* makes quite clear that the process of creating and serving meals, even before a household became officially »royal«, was a mammoth task requiring a great deal of equipment.[10] It is significant that Platter clearly perceives the opportunity to watch this sophisticated and undoubtedly impressive if ultimately abstract ritual as a signal honour. In fact, that admittance even to the chamber concerned was restricted to gentlemen or above demonstrates the importance of eating to social stratification, in a court where strict delineations were anxiously maintained, viewed as essential for sociopolitical stability.

Perhaps the dining ritual's most significant feature is the obvious one, its abstraction: this attention is lavished on merely the representative act of the Queen's consumption, rather than the actuality, which took place »privily«. At no time is the queen herself glimpsed, let alone watched in the act of consumption. Gestures of respect habitually accorded a monarch – genuflection, bowing – are offered instead to the empty table, »the same obeisance and honours performed as if the Queen herself had sat there.« Moreover, the ritual itself serves to reinforce hierarchies. The invisible queen gets first refusal of everything, before the food is carried back out to the lords' table. True power, it would appear, lies not in dramatic consumption but in sufficient resources to refuse it. (Accordingly, Elizabeth's successor James I would display a lavish banquet and then dispose of it, so another, even more indulgent example could be served.[11]) That modern Western plenty and conspicuous consumption has brought in its wake an intense focus on the dramatically thin body and the growth of anorexia presents an intriguing counterpoint. That (perceived) power or control is attained through the refusal of abundant resources and the suppression of physical desires, the rejection or refusal of need despite the opportunity for its satisfaction, is an im-

10 J. L. McIntosh, *From Heads of Household to Heads of State: The Preaccession Households of Mary and Elizabeth Tudor, 1516 – 1558*, New York: Columbia University Press, 2009.

11 Sarah Gristwood, *Arbella: England's Lost Queen*, London: Bantam, 2003, p. 308.

portant point of connection between contemporary sufferers of anorexia and early modern self-starvers, whose manifestation of this particular characteristic could potentially be described as »proto-anorexic«.[12] Accordingly, of course, the audience Platter joined were not offered food at all; no right of either acceptance or refusal was granted them. Simply witnessing the mealtime of those sufficiently elevated to dine at the Queen's expense is a considerable »honour«, as Platter points out. The absent Queen's consumption is lavish in metaphor, and thus signals superiority over those lesser nobles who must physically demonstrate it, whilst simultaneously being abstemious in reality and thus enabling the iconography of impenetrability and imperviousness to human hungers that served several ideological purposes for Elizabeth I.

It is striking, accordingly, how few representations of Elizabeth actually eating exist. William Camden, albeit writing some time after her death, and perhaps keen to imply a critical contrast with the lavish consumption of James I's court, insists she ate abstemiously, rarely, and only when prompted by hunger:

> The Queene her selfe [...] alwaies liued in perfect health, (for she neuer ate but when she had a stomacke, neither drunke any Wine.[13]

Nugae Antiquae contains one letter from Robert Sidney to Harington, written in 1600, in which he focuses on the »honour« done him by the Queen's willingness to eat in his home: »she did vouchsafe to eat two morsels of rich comfit cake, and drank a small cordial from a gold cup.«[14] Generously, Sidney (truthfully or otherwise) seeks to transfer this honour: she also »hath tasted your [Harington's] dainties, and saith you have marvellous skill in cooking of good fruits.«[15] Significant as this is, its mention, the meagreness of the (by now aging) Queen's consumption, its apparent rarity, and the emphasis placed on the honour Elizabeth is

12 See, e. g., Helen Malson, *The Thin Woman: Feminism, Post-Structuralism and the Social Psychology of Anorexia Nervosa*, London: Routledge, 1997; Joan Jacobs Brumberg, *Fasting Girls: The History of Anorexia Nervosa*, London: Vintage Books, 2000; Susan Bordo, *Unbearable Weight. Feminism, Western Culture, and the Body*, Berkeley, CA, University of California Press, 2003.

13 William Camden, *Annales the true and royall history of the famous empresse Elizabeth Queene of England France and Ireland &c....* , London 1625, Book 2, p. 317.

14 »Sir Robert Sydney to Sir John Harington, 1600«, in: John Harington, Henry Harington (eds.), *Nugae Antiquae: being a miscellaneous collection of Original Papers in prose and verse; written during the reigns of Henry VIII Edward VI Queen Mary Elizabeth and King James*, London 1804, I., p. 315. There are interesting resonances here with Jonson's »To Penshurst« as a celebration of Robert Sidney's hospitality to James I, and an example of the use of food to symbolise aristocratic largesse and social order. See »The Forest: ii. To Penshurst« in: Ben Jonson, *The Works of Ben Jonson. With a biographical memoir by William Gifford*, Boston: Phillips, Sampson, &Co., 1853, pp. 801-802.

15 Harington (as note 14), I., p. 312.

doing Sidney all underline the importance of such an occasion. Further, it raises a number of questions. Is that all the Queen ate? For how long? Was that a meal to Elizabeth? Given that elsewhere in the letter Sidney highlights the mutuality of this food exchange by describing his own sustenance from the »Queens kitchen« (»I supp broth from the Queens kitchen, and eat of her Majesties sweet cakes, which do nourish my poor blood, and cherish goodhumours.«) and the Queen's journey back to the palace, it is clear that she had her own kitchens and staff at her disposal. Any form of food exchange with the queen apparently represents a signal honour, and it is tempting to suggest she used such a gesture of intimacy and favour to gather support from the influential Sidneys, and presumably other households that she visited on progress and at other times.[16]

Elsewhere, Harington also perceives the Queen's food choices as a political issue, and one highlighted by the paucity of her consumption; he describes with some pride her preference for Lady Harington's sweetmeats, and the resulting ill-feeling among her ladies as sufficient to prevent »my Mall« sending any more. Elizabeth »tasted my wife's comfits, and [...] moche praised her cunninge in the makinge. – Sende no more, for other ladies jealousie workethe againste my Mall's comfits, and this will not comforte her –« Harington is undoubtedly somewhat preoccupied with food, referring frequently to his diet or others', and using food as an ideological metaphor (a yearning for peaceful domestic and non-political existence, for instance, is indicated by »eat[ing] Aldborne rabbits, and get[ting] fish (as you recommend) from the man at Curry-Rival...«), but nevertheless it is clear that Elizabeth's food choices could be a powerful means of indicating favour or disfavour amongst courtiers.[17]

At court, where even minute details of food supply and service could be carried out to precise monarchical instruction, eating in privacy was easier to achieve, and so perhaps the paucity of representations of Elizabeth eating isn't surprising. But even on progress or outdoors, in an admittedly performative »holiday« mode, few if any accounts of »feasts and banquettes« mention the Queen herself actually partaking, focusing instead on the lavish hospitality offered her. Whilst timing is often signalled by reference to mealtimes – »after dinner« or »before supper« – this serves a temporal and geographical function rather than offering a glimpse of the Queen at the table.[18] Two extant accounts remain of her 1578 progress through Norfolk and Suffolk, Bernard Garter's *The*

16 Ibid., I., p. 314.

17 From »Notes and Remembraunces«, in: Harington (as note 14), I, p. 166-167; and to Sir Hugh Portman, ibid., I, pp. 318-319.

18 See, e. g., Thomas Churchyard, *A Discourse of the Queenes Maiesties entertainement in Suffolk and Norfolk* ..., London: Henry Bynneman, [1578]; Bernard Garter, *The Ioyfvll Receyuing of the Queenes most excellent Maiestie into hir Highnesse Citie of Norvvich*, London 1578; Harington (as note 14).

Ioyfvll Receyuing of the Queenes most excellent Maiestie into hir Highnesse Citie of Norvvich and Thomas Churchyard's *A Discourse of the Queenes Maiesties entertainement in Suffolk and Norfolk.* Garter never alludes to food or feasting, mentioning mealtimes only to situate a masque or event temporally (»after dinner«) while Churchyard refers repeatedly to local landowners »feasting« the Queen's train, or the French ambassadors, with no discussion of the Queen herself.[19] »Feasting« in this context is obviously an opportunity for public recognition and display of local prosperity and resources, naming local gentry or describing their achievements (»a most rare and delicate Dinner and Banquette«) possibly as much a matter of patronage or position-consolidation as recognition of culinary expertise.[20] Interestingly, the active subject of the verb »feasting« belongs not to those eating, but to those providing the meal; its consumers are marginalised.

Illustration from George Turberville, *The Noble Arte of Venerie* (London 1575)

19 Churchyard (as note 18), sigs B4r, E3r, G4r.
20 Ibid., sigs E3r, B3v, B4r, G4r.

To »feast« is not an act of consumption, but provision.[21] The Queen's personal consumption – never mentioned, let alone described – is clearly irrelevant compared to the provision of sufficient food to »feast« her followers and display of the resources necessary to do so. Symbolic or potential consumption – entitlement to vast and elaborate meals – signalled majesty in the public eye, regardless of the monarch in question's actual habits. A similar elision of actual royal eating is evident in George Turberville's 1575 *Noble Arte of Venerie.* Despite its extensive instructions on correct methods and menus for a royal or aristocratic picnic, and an accompanying picture of Elizabeth seated on a chair amid a forest feast, nowhere is there suggestion of the honoured guest partaking.[22]

As long as Elizabeth could demonstrate her power through assumed entitlement to lavish banquets and her hosts theirs by providing them, whether or not she actually chose to eat them appears entirely secondary.

Starvation and strategy

Throughout her life, Elizabeth could be seen using food and the iconographic potential of her body to signal, express and negotiate traumatic experience and political difficulty. Even in her infancy, the tension between regimes symbolised by rivalry between the king's daughters in their new combined household was played out in terms of alternative timing and substance of food intake, considerably increasing household expenditure.[23] Whilst at this point Elizabeth was clearly too young to be exercising any independent authority, Mary's presence or absence at mealtimes and the conflict between the households must have been noticeable enough to influence her nascent understanding.

Moreover, changes in her weight and eating patterns were noted and commented on by those around her, and perceived as an indicator of her state of

21 The OED describes both these usages as dating from c. 1300, its first examples for »partaking« being »c. 1300« and 1385, for »providing« being 1340 – 1370 and 1377. Certainly both senses were centuries old at this point. Intriguingly, a further usage »to feast away« as in »to drive away by feasting« appeared in 1606, less than 40 years after these accounts were published. »feast, v.« *OED Online*, Oxford: Oxford University Press, March 2011. <http://www.oed.com/viewdictionaryentry/Entry/68800>.

22 George Turberville, *The Noble Arte of Venerie or Hunting. Wherein is handled and set out the Vertues, Nature, and Properties of fiuetene sundrie Chaces togither, with the order and maner how to Hunte and kill euery one of them. Translated and collected* ..., London 1575, see pp. 90-93.

23 See previous chapter. *Letters & Papers,* Vol. 8, p. 172, 25 March 1535. See also *State Papers Online*, 19 Apr. 2011, also 440: »Expenses of the Princess's household ...«. See also Eustace Chapuys, »Chapuys to Charles V«, in: *Letters & Papers,* Vol. 7, p. 142, 17 March 1534. *State Papers Online*. Web. 21 Apr. 2011.

mind and political attitudes. At the beginning of her reign, during the political minefield caused by Katherine Grey's clandestine marriage, rumours about the Earl of Leicester and his wife's death, and possible marriages of Mary Queen of Scots, the Spanish Bishop Álvaro de la Quadra wrote to his king that Elizabeth's »dropsical« and »extremely thin« body was a matter of national concern:

> What is of most importance now, as I am informed, is that the Queen is becoming dropsical and has already began to swell extraordinarily. I have been advised of this from three different sources and by a person who has the opportunity of being an eye witness. To all appearance she is falling away, and is extremely thin and the colour of a corpse. I do not know whether the coming of this Swede is in consequence of any news he may have received of this malady of the Queen's, but I do know that the marchioness of Northampton, who is in a better position to judge than anyone else, is very intimate with the Swedish ambassador, and has received valuable presents from him. That the Marchioness and Lady Cobham consider the Queen in a dangerous condition is beyond doubt, and if they are mistaken I am mistaken also.[24]

This highlights the importance of the Queen's body in interpreting and discussing England's figurative political security and position. In more ways than one, the Queen's body represented the national body, the security and safety of the realm

24 Martin A. S. Hume (ed.), »Simancas: September 1561«, in: *Calendar of State Papers, Spain (Simancas)*, (hereafter *CSP Spanish*) Vol. 1: 1558 – 1567 (1892), pp. 212-217, *British History Online*, Web. 02 May 2011, <http://www.british-history.ac.uk/report.aspx?compid=86733&strquery=> »The Swede« in question is probably King Eric XIV of Sweden (13 December 1533 – 26 February 1577), whose sister Princess Cecilia of Sweden, second-eldest daughter of King Gustav I, came to England in 1565 to negotiate her half-brother Eric's marriage to Elizabeth. Assuming the dating of the letter is correct, the Marchionness of Northampton in question was Elizabeth Brooke (25 June 1526 – 2 April 1565), wife of William Parr Marquess of Northampton, notoriously favoured by Elizabeth until her death in 1565. Five years afterwards, Parr remarried; the new Marchioness was one of Cecilia's attendants and Elizabeth's ladies-in-waiting, Helena Ulfsdotter Snakenborg (c. 1549 – 10 April 1635) who also became very close to the Queen. Frances Newton, Lady Cobham (1539 – 17 October 1592), second wife of Sir William Brooke, 10th Baron Cobham, was another of Elizabeth's closest attendants. Leanda de Lisle, *Sisters Who Would be Queen: The Tragedy of Mary, Katherine and Lady Jane Grey*, London: Harpercollins, 2010, p. 219; see also 348n, reports this as the Scots ambassador William Maitland during the succession crisis of 1567 due to Katherine's pregnancy, quoting »To all appearances … falling away … extremely thin and the colour of a corpse« as from *CSP Spanish*, Vol I, 1558 – 1567, p. 214. I have been unable to verify this reference, but it is entirely possible that Maitland sent a similar report. Incongruous as »swelling extraordinarily« and »extremely thin« may appear, it seems likely that this might indicate a bloated stomach and emaciated limbs and other areas.

contingent on her specific physical health and continuance.[25] The apparent direct impact of stress-induced inedia, therefore, was a matter of national concern. There is an evocative description of Elizabeth after the Essex debacle in a letter from John Harington to Hugh Portman which reads:

> She is quite disfavourd, and unattird, and *these troubles waste her muche*. She disregardeth every costlie cover that cometh to the table, and taketh little but manchet and succory potage. Every new message from the city doth disturb her, and she frowns on all the ladies.[26]

Elizabeth's pointed food behaviour – and her courtiers' keen observation of it – have significant implications. Whether accurately or otherwise, inedia is widely interpreted as a direct emotional response to current events. Although Quadra had not personally witnessed the state of the Queen's body, he had heard of it from »three different sources« as well as »a person who has the opportunity of being an eye witness«. Even amongst those habitually denied the Queen's presence or the long-distance sight of her person, changes in her body or eating habits were discussed avidly and reported internationally, scoured minutely for indications of intentions, feelings, responses or possible political moves. (Not to mention implications of her gynaecological health and fertility, a matter of intense political import at least into the 1580s.)[27] Those in closest proximity to her were courted and themselves watched closely, for political allegiance, personal response and possible implications for domestic and European politics (the Marchioness of Northampton and her mysterious connection with the Swedish ambassador for example, here reported to the King of Spain, became a matter of international concern, partly because of her rank but largely because of her intimacy with Elizabeth).

For the latter to visibly »disregard every costlie cover« that came to the table, therefore, restricting herself to bread (manchet) and succory pottage (chicory stew, particularly abstemious given chicory's bitterness and perceived medicinal

25 In fact, Leonard Tennenhouse asserts that »[Elizabeth] constantly encouraged an equation to be made between the health of her body, its wellbeing and integrity, and that of the state.« Leonard Tennenhouse, »Violence done to women on the Renaissance stage«, in: Nancy Armstrong, Leonard Tennenhouse (eds.), *The Violence of Representation: literature and the history of violence,* London: Routledge, 1989. See also Peter Stallybrass, »Patriarchal Territories«, in: Margaret W. Ferguson, Maureen Quilligan, Nancy Vickers (eds.) *Rewriting the Renaissance: The Discourses of Sexual Difference in Early Modern Europe*, Chicago: University of Chicago Press, 1986, pp. 23-45; Helen Hackett, *Virgin Mother, Maiden Queen: Elizabeth I and the Cult of the Virgin Mary*, Hampshire and London: Macmillan, 1995.

26 Harington (as note 14), Vol. 1, p. 317, 9 Oct 1601, emphasis mine.

27 Carole Levin, *The Heart and Stomach of a King: Elizabeth I and the Politics of Sex and Power*, Philadelphia: University of Pennsylvania Press, 1994.

qualities) was to make a paradoxically public statement of distress, signalling to the world her dissatisfaction with Essex's or Grey's behaviour, raising the implicitly threatening spectre of her own ill health and consequent instability, and in some manner justifying the perceived harshness of her treatment of the rebels, underlining the importance of political resolution for the realm. Presumably formal dining ritual continued unabated, despite an obvious decrease in the Queen's personal food consumption. This could represent either a proto-anorexic need to impose directly physically perceptible control on one of the few variables offering the opportunity to do so (entirely compatible with the literal insecurity of Elizabeth's position and metaphorical insecurity of her identity at this time), or a physiological response to greater stress. Either way, it was evidently not considered a positive step: prompted by unhappy psychological reality and outward circumstance, rather than an approved means of denying feminine sensuality.

Her food-restriction and its physical consequences, despite the relative privacy of her actual food intake, were performed in court before influential people well aware of ongoing power wrangles and the possible impacts of Grey's marriage or Essex's rebellion. Deliberately altering her diet in direct response to Essex's betrayal publicly displayed distress and damage both to Elizabeth herself and to the monarchy manifest in her, offering explanation for and defence of the severe punishment he suffered as a consequence. Moreover, as the letters attest, courtiers watched closely for such »signs« of response. A second letter, from Harington to his wife, describes Elizabeth herself deliberately drawing attention to this process and the meanings of her restricted diet. Harington reports her as saying:

> When thou doste feele creepinge tyme at thye gate, these fooleries will please thee lesse; I am paste my relishe for such matters: thou seeste my bodilie meate dothe not suite me well; I have eaten but one ill tastede cake since yesternighte.[28]

Whilst we have no means of confirming these as Elizabeth's exact words, whether they represent her perspective or Harington's inference the salient point – that Elizabeth's visible reduction in food intake and consequent thinness was used as a means of political communication, and interpreted as such – remains. It is noticeable that Elizabeth plays down her own agency here, drawing attention instead to the inevitable effects of »creeping tyme«, reinforcing her »lack of relishe« by emphasising the single »ill tastede« cake that she has eaten. Whether she means to imply that the cake tasted ill to her, or she was able only to »taste« (as in eat) it »ill« (not very well or very much), the underlying implication is that Elizabeth's body, not a conscious mind notable for its political canniness, is responsible for the »[much] wasting« Harington describes. This constructs her

28 Harington (as note 14), Vol. 1, p. 323: Harington to his wife, 17 Dec 1602.

meagre diet as an unwilled, direct result of »these troubles« instead of either a conscious attempt to cope with them or a self-directed means of implicit political threat, with the handy side effect of diverting attention from the Earl of Essex's theatrical suffering.[29]

Such performances and attitudes participated in, perpetuated and appealed to a general rhetoric of the female body as essentially uncontrollable, related to humoral theory and its conceptualisation of feminine physicality as essentially more permeable, moist and liquid than the masculine equivalent.[30] That women's bodies – particularly aging women's bodies – were customarily represented as beyond their control, capable of undermining or disintegrating forms of social or even magical power possessed in other contexts, adds an additional dimension to the Queen's ostentatiously restrained, controlled behaviour, not to mention the intense scrutiny and continual reinterpretation to which her body was subject.[31] On one level repudiating any stereotypical femininity, by obliquely signalling towards a misogynistic cultural truism and applying it to herself, Elizabeth is also diverting attention away from her other contextual identities, cunning politician and gender-neutral monarchical body politic, and underlining her apolitical feminine body and emotional vulnerability. It was an ideological manoeuvre she performed many times over the course of her reign with considerable success.

Gender, appetite, anatomy and ambiguity

Much of Elizabeth's political rhetoric hinged on separating her »body politic« from the »weak and feeble woman['s]« physical body she possessed.[32] In her very first speech at Hatfield, she deliberately distinguished her »one body naturally considered« from the »body politic to govern« in the »office« to which she had

29 Paul Hammond, »The Smiling Crocodile: the Earl of Essex and Late Elizabethan Popularity«, in: Peter Lake, Stephen Pincus (eds.), *The Politics of the Public Sphere in Early Modern England*, Manchester: Manchester University Press, 2007.

30 See, e. g., Gail Kern Paster, *The Body Embarrassed: Drama and the Disciplines of Shame in Early Modern England*, Ithaca, NY: Cornell University Press, 1993; Diane Purkiss, *The Witch in History: Early Modern and Twentieth-Century Representations*, London: Routledge, 1996.

31 See Kern Paster (as note 30), especially Introduction, »Leaky Vessels«, pp. 1-64.

32 Elizabeth I, *Elizabeth I: Collected Works*, ed. Leah S. Marcus, Janel Mueller, Mary Beth Rose, London: University of Chicago Press, 2000, p. 52 and p. 322. There is, however, scholarly disagreement over whether or not these are her actual words. See Susan Frye, *Elizabeth I and the Politics of Representation*, Oxford: Oxford University Press, 1996; Levin (as note 27), chapter 6. Regardless of their accuracy or otherwise, the phrase undoubtedly (as Levin puts it) »characterizes some of the struggles, contradictions, and cultural anxieties that dominated the collective consciousness of England« during Elizabeth's reign. (Ibid., back cover.)

been called by »His heavenly will«.[33] Similarly, whilst she occasionally apologises for the perceived inadequacies of her biological sex, she continually follows such apologies with reinforcement of the masculinity of her assumed office.[34] Frequently, Elizabeth emphasises negative contemporary feminine stereotypes, applying them directly to her physical self. Yet this simply enables her to differentiate more strongly the masculinised »princely«, »kingly« body politic from which she also speaks and through which she claims her authority.[35] In the dining ritual, it is the office of the body politic, the invisible and emblematic monarch at the head of the table, who is served; what Elizabeth herself chooses to eat behind the scenes or otherwise is rendered largely irrelevant. It is the representative consumption rather than its actuality which becomes the point. Because the »body politic« is primarily envisaged as masculine, even quantitatively the vast staged and ultimately symbolic consumption of the banqueting ceremony becomes appropriate. Writing to James VI, Elizabeth repeatedly figured herself as »king«, describing herself as a »strange king [to the Scots]«, or explicitly asserting »though a King I be ...«.[36] This probably indicates a determination to assert her equality with James, but that she needed to do so by essentially denying the existence of her gender in the context of political capacity is undoubtedly salient. Even in her public speeches, the frequency with which Elizabeth refers to herself as »prince« rather than any other monarchal honorific serves to emphasize the extent to which she presented her authoritative, monarchal self as potentially masculinised, or at least androgynous.[37]

That such gender ambiguity was intrinsic not only to Elizabeth's own self-presentation but to others' perceptions of her is evident in both published work and private letters, to an extent that occasionally exceeded even her own consciously-stated androgyny. Nobles such as the Earls of Shrewsbury and Essex, as well as William Cecil, referred to her in masculine terms: in 1574 Shrewsbury told his son Gilbert that

33 Elizabeth I (as note 32), p. 52.

34 Ibid., p. 70.

35 The question of the Queen's Two Bodies has been comprehensively discussed: following Ernst Kantorowicz's 1957 *The King's Two Bodies: A Study in Mediaeval Political Theology* (reprinted New Jersey: Princeton University Press, 1997) and Marie Axton's *The Queen's Two Bodies: Drama and the Elizabethan Succession*, London: Royal Historical Society, 1977; Frye (as note 32).

36 Elizabeth to James, July 6, 1590, in: Elizabeth I (as note 32), p. 365; Elizabeth I to James VI, 21 August 1600, in: *The Letters of Queen Elizabeth,* ed. G. B. Harrison (1935), New York: Funk & Wagnalls, 1968, pp. 278-279.

37 See Elizabeth I (as note 32), e. g. p. 70, 95, 105, 106, 108, etc; also Hackett (as note 25), pp. 99-100, 115-19, 127, 180, 240; Levin (as note 27), passim, esp. pp. 90-148.

> I hope you will be faithful [...] to the Queen's Majesty, my Sovereign, who to me, under God, is King of Kings and Lord of Lords.[38]

As Susan Frye succinctly points out at the beginning of her *Elizabeth I: The Competition for Representation*, the enduring image of Elizabeth in armour haranguing her troops at Tilbury is almost certainly fictitious. However, William Camden's account nevertheless emphasises her »masculine Spirit«,

> riding about through the Ranks of Armed men drawn up on both sides her, with a Leader's Truncheon in her Hand, sometimes with a martial Pace, another while gently like a Woman, incredible it is how much she encouraged the hearts of her Captains and Soldiers by her Presence and Speech to them.[39]

It is clear here that Camden uses Elizabeth's queenly gender ambiguity as a strength, exploiting the distinction between the Queen's martial role and a typical feminine one to emphasise the impact of both upon the soldiers. Dining ceremony enabled a similar duality, offering the spectacle of consumption whilst enabling the Queen herself to eat sufficiently sparingly to maintain her strikingly slender outline. It also served to assert a certain amount of independence from subjects, ambassadors and counsellors, all of whom would only witness her dining if explicitly invited to do so. (However, it did grant those ladies-in-waiting who habitually served the Queen at table a commensurate amount of privilege, which could bring its own problems.)

Sanctity, symbolism and shared consumption

Further, ritual has a curiously parallel effect, serving both to assert the authority of the monarchal body politic, and to underline the potentially fragile dependence of this authority on ceremony and iconography. Functioning both as symbol and sanctification, it perhaps recalls the elements of pre-Reformation church ceremonial retained in Elizabeth's Anglican settlement, or even Catholic church ritual; highlighting the importance of such elements in conveying authority and importance, whilst also perhaps providing an alternative focus for them. Here, the dining ceremony underlines the significance of iconographic and symbolic manipulation to the image of monarchy. Meanwhile, it highlights the importance of food as matter: the connection between food and royal body is perversely reinforced by the transposition of food for monarch as subject of reverence, reinforcing the phenomenological truism that eating is assimilation.

38 See ibid., p. 123.
39 Camden (as note 13), p. 326.

What enters (or is intended to enter) the monarch's body here shares – or to be more precise, is given by the ritual itself and thus adopts – her divinity even before the moment of absorption, »the same obeisance and honours« accorded it »as if the Queen herself were there«. It is hard not to make comparisons with the Eucharist, that other foodstuff elevated by ceremony to sacred status, and posit Elizabeth as offering in some sense a secular version of Communion ritual that actually focused attention on the monarch as a God's representative on earth. While the monarch's food becomes the Host, by implication the royal person not only dines on divinity, but comes to represent a mediator between God and subjects.[40]

Roy Strong's *The Cult of Elizabeth* suggests that much of the imagery surrounding the Queen was »skilfully created to buttress public order and, even more, deliberately to replace the pre-Reformation externals of religion«; dining ritual could easily be fitted into that category.[41] Whilst Helen Hackett has disputed Strong's rather simplified and celebratory treatment, emphasising instead the complex iconographic compromises and political motivations involved in Elizabethan appropriations of quasi-Catholic symbols and rituals, it is likely that not to be seen eating in public could have reinforced the quasi-divinity of Elizabeth's self-representation, just as her abstemious consumption could be seen to emphasise engagement with higher, intellectual, spiritual matters rather than the base concerns of the flesh. Susan Frye posits that towards the end of her reign, she increasingly claimed her authority from this unique interpolating position between her subjects and God. Faced by the inevitable aging process, both Elizabeth herself and those around her faced the concomitant necessity of presenting an increasingly culturally denigrated form – her undeniably feminine body, no longer fertile or conforming to culturally prescribed notions of beauty – as a fit vessel for political authority. It is therefore unsurprising that an increasingly symbolic and spiritual means of presentation, uniting chastity with the eternal and ageless to distance the queen from the fallibly human flesh, became apparent.[42] But right from the start of her reign, she consistently presented herself as occupying a unique and divinely ordained position as mediator between subjects and deity:

40 This reflects many and complex elements of early modern religious symbolism: to name but a few, the Protestant notion of the godly ruler, the Catholic concepts of sainthood (in particular the Virgin Mary, see Helen Hackett [as note 25]) and a (celibate) elevated priesthood.

41 Roy Strong, *The Cult of Elizabeth: Elizabethan Portraiture and Pageantry*, London: Thames & Hudson, 1977, p. 16; Hackett (as note 25).

42 Susan Frye, *Elizabeth I: The Competition for Representation*, Oxford: Oxford University Press, 1997, pp. 111-114; see also Hackett (as note 25), pp. 163-201.

> I am God's creature, ordained to obey His appointment, I will thereto yield, desiring from the bottom of my heart that I may have assistance of His grace to be the minister of His heavenly will in this office now committed to me.[43]

That she is specifically set apart by God, »ordained« to be »by his permission a body politic to govern« is considerably reinforced by the invisibility of her eating practices. Whilst, as befits a ruler of Elizabeth's sheer canniness, this can be seen to conform to a Protestant and specifically Calvinist model of the secular ruler as God's chosen agent on earth, as well as to a Catholic model of the intercessory saint, in either case, her apparent immunity to the bodily necessities which preoccupied her subjects underlines the concept of a connection with the divine. Whilst Elizabeth went on progress throughout her reign, limited only by her physical capacity, even those who saw her would primarily have done so from a distance in carefully staged circumstances. For the vast majority of her subjects she would still have been chiefly visible through published texts and visual media, conceptualised essentially as an icon whose presentation could be at least partially controlled; for such basic human functions as eating, sleeping and so on to be invisible not only asserted privilege, in an age where the vast majority had little privacy, but contributed to the created image of a separate, quasi-divine, iconic being.

Power, politics and penetration

Further, in its assumption of a controlling, observant position, watching or describing the Queen's eating both witnesses and constitutes in itself the symbolic invasion of her body, emphasising the vulnerability inherent in her feminine penetrability and the power of the male voice describing it. Those watching her eat, especially if not doing so themselves, observe a penetration of the Queen's bodily limits; for the Queen to eat in private acts as a primitive form of defence. The necessity of eating – pabular penetration – is intrinsic to the human body, and mirrors the sexual act. That, therefore, the impermeability of her body's limits was hugely significant to Elizabeth's self-construction as a Virgin Queen is hardly a revelation, and has been explored in great detail elsewhere.[44] Andrew and Catherine Belsey's essay on »Icons of Divinity«: makes a direct comparison with representations of Henry VIII, noting that:

43 Elizabeth I (as note 32), p. 52.

44 See, e. g., Hackett (as note 25); Frye (as note 42); Phillipa Berry, *Of Chastity and Power: Elizabethan Literature and the Unmarried Queen*, London: Routledge, 1989), esp. pp. 1-38, 61-83, 111 ff.

> In the sixteenth century [...] because of the cultural constructions of gender, an emphasis on the character of the female body connotes something quite different: not authority but availability, not sovereignty but subjection. Where Henry's right to dominate is confirmed by his virility, represented in that extraordinarily prominent codpiece, Elizabeth depends by contrast on sexuality subdued, on the self-containment and self-control of the Virgin Queen [...] in the place corresponding to Henry's codpiece [...] Elizabeth displays a giant pearl [...] a succession of pearls [between groin and headdress] emphasis[e] a link between majesty and virginity. The juxtaposition [...] displays the Queen impregnable [...] powerful to precisely the degree she is inviolable.[45]

But that the resistance to sexual penetration implicitly encoded in the iconography of sieves, phoenixes, pearls and other representations of virginity was reflected in a commensurate refusal to be pabularly penetrated has been less comprehensively addressed. It is unsurprising that the sensual penetration that is eating was witnessed only by intimates, since in a culture whose stability depended on masculine regulation of what penetrated the female body and justified such regulation by a fundamental and all-pervasive association of the feminine with unregulated appetite, to be publicly invulnerable to physical hungers represented a peculiarly feminine form of power. Thus the conjunction of impenetrability and femininity Elizabeth projected in some ways reinforced her royal authority and apartness, her quasi-divinity.

This is particularly salient given that her femininity was culturally extremely problematic. That her rule followed the more-or-less disastrously unstable reigns of Jane Grey and Mary Tudor doubtless exacerbated already extant anxieties about the fitness of a woman's monarchal authority. Her sister's unpopular Catholicism had been coupled with a politically catastrophic marriage and, perhaps most importantly, serious reproductive difficulties, to offer a significant public space to critics of female monarchy.[46] The assumed instability of female rule was partially mitigated by Elizabeth's Protestantism, but still in a predominantly patriarchal society the inferred need for a husband to facilitate the production of heirs led to understandable concerns about his identity, particularly so if his masculinity was to imply a degree of authority over the monarch in keeping with contemporary marriage ideology.[47] As J. L. McIntosh pointed out, »Until Henry took steps to disinherit Mary in 1527, England's foreign and domestic policy centred on

45 Andrew Belsey, Catherine Belsey, »Icons of Divinity: Portraits of Elizabeth I«, in: Lucy Gent and Nigel Llewellyn (eds.), *Renaissance Bodies: The Human Figure in English Culture c. 1540 – 1660*, London: Reaktion, 1990.

46 E. g., John Knox, *First Blast of the Trumpet Against the Monstrous Regiment of Women* (1558).

47 Norman Jones, *Birth of the Elizabethan age: England in the 1560s*, Oxford: Blackwell, 1993, p. 5.

ensuring that Mary wedded a man who could either credibly claim the throne himself or possessed enough political stature to rule England as Mary's husband«, and much of Elizabeth's politics, at least until she passed childbearing age, was concerned with negotiating the possibility of marriage.[48] Susan Doran, among many others, has explored in detail the machinations of her complex courtships; she suggests that Elizabeth's failure to marry in fact stemmed initially from a lack of ultimately suitable candidates rather than a conscious decision.[49]

Whether or not this is the case, it is certain that whatever decision Elizabeth made would be ideologically difficult. As has been explored numerous times elsewhere, the demands mid-sixteenth-century ideology made of monarchs and of women (particularly married ones) could be problematically incompatible. To start from the obvious, ideal femininity involved submission and acceptance of greater authority: the antithesis of a monarch's role. In her impermeability, however, Elizabeth manifested an ideal of virginal femininity fundamentally incompatible with the cultural demands made of adult womanhood. A chaste and sealed vessel, impervious to assault or penetration, was ideal only as a preliminary stage to ultimate possession by a man. Whilst the Church of England never venerated virginity to the extent common in pre-Reformation Catholicism, post-Reformation ideology retained a certain amount of implied reverence for the concept, more as the necessary prelude to standard reproductive femininity than a productive end in itself. Ultimately, the exercise of power as a woman necessitated union with, and thus supposedly submission to, a man. The concept of »companionate marriage« based on affection, with the husband as guide and mentor, was beginning to emerge, and yet such ideals were obviously incompatible with Elizabeth's sovereign monarchy. In general, England perceived the need for a string of lusty heirs to provide dynastic security. But when said lusty heirs become potentially the sons of either a foreign prince whose principal allegiance (and thus whose children's potential allegiance) was elsewhere (as had been the case with Mary's husband, largely absent Philip) or a native aristocrat already enmeshed in the complex factional rivalries of court (like Jane Grey's union with Guilford Dudley) the question became a lot more complicated. However, whatever the particular controversy raging at any one time, it always centred on the troublesome reproductive capacity of Elizabeth's inconveniently feminine body.

48 McIntosh (as note 10), conclusion, p. 7. See, e. g. Susan Doran, *Monarchy and Matrimony*, London: HarperCollins, 1993.

49 Doran (as note 48).

Inside Elizabeth

Accordingly, all aspects of her bodily functions, however intimate, were the subject of prurient interest on both a national and an international level. Ambassadors, reports sent to the Spanish, Venetian and French courts demonstrate that Elizabeth's menstruation was not only a subject of absorbing interest but also problematically irregular, something which even if not prompted by low bodyweight would have been considerably exacerbated thereby. According to modern biographers, ambassadors deliberately sought out this information, bribing Elizabeth's servants.[50] Certainly rumours about physical, psychological or physiological infirmity abounded.

Il Schifanoya, the Venetian ambassador, wrote to his Mantuan counterpart Ottaviano Vivalino that

> before leaving her majesty was blooded from one foot and from one arm, but what her infirmity is, is not known. Many persons say things which I should not dare to write.[51]

The Spanish ambassador muttered similarly darkly that:

> If my spies do not lie, which I believe they do not, for a certain reason which they have lately given me I understand she will not bear children, but if the Archduke is a man, even if she die without any, he will be able to keep the kingdom without the support of your majesty.[52]

(It is worthwhile noting here how the possession of effective ruling authority and masculinity are assumed to be synonymous. The one is figured as the other. One can see Elizabeth's problem.) Their Roman counterpart is more specific, if not necessarily more convincing:

> They say that she has hardly ever had the purgations proper to all women, but that instead nature has come to the rescue by establishing an issue in one of her legs, which has never been scant of flow but the Queen has fallen ill, and at present seems to be quite dried up, nor know the physicians how to find a remedy for this mishap.[53]

This reveals not only the intense scrutiny under which Elizabeth lived (something of which she was well aware, declaring quite accurately that »my life is in the open, and I have so many witnesses that I cannot understand how bad [...] jud-

50 See, e. g., Weir (as note 2), pp. 47 ff.; Levin (as note 27).
51 *CSP Venetian*, Vol. 1, p. 105.
52 *CSP Spanish*, Vol. 1, p. 63.
53 *CSP Rome*, Vol. II, p. 363.

gement can have been formed of me«[54]), but also intense disquiet at the image of an inviolable, sealed woman, free even of the menstruation that according to humoral theory literally manifested feminine inferiority. If socially acceptable femininity depended on women as liquid, moist, unsealed vessels, subject to appetite and desire and masculine penetration to function, then it is hardly surprising that the Virgin Queen carefully minimised the public transgression and permeability of her bodily limits, especially if her royal authority partially hinged on self-representation as an iconic, semi-divine spiritual leader rather than an emphatically earthly woman.

It is no surprise that contemporaries seeking to denigrate Elizabeth did so almost universally in terms of not only femininity but penetrability, hinging on sexual incontinence or dysfunctionality. Contemporary critics rewrote the apartness from traditional womanhood she sought effectively to project right back into customary negative templates of an unruly femininity which was nevertheless ultimately subject to masculine penetration and authority. (After all, to have »shamefully ... defiled her person and cuntry [sic]«, »by this damnable and detestable art [of seduction, in this case of Robert Dudley Earl of Leicester, among other ›favourites‹] to [have] intangle[d] in sinne, and overthrowe the ... nobility and gentry of the land« as Cardinal William Allen declares, requires said »nobility and gentry« to have actively engaged in penetration of the Queen's body and all the dominance that implied.[55]) Intense focus on the distinctively feminine features of the Queen's physicality and selfhood challenged the ideological and symbolic distance she maintained from her subjects: the dining ritual, underlining such distances, helped to maintain it. Conscious control over what entered her body, her public food intake, obviously counterbalanced an overly prurient focus on its supposedly uncontrollable productivity of which she was well aware. Outsiders sought to enter Elizabeth's body in order to fathom its reproductive secrets; it is hardly surprising she countered such assumed invasion with a refusal to admit outsiders to watch the literal penetration of her body at mealtimes. It is worth noting that her successor, James, made a point of differentiating himself by offering open access: »anyone may enter the King's presence while he is at dinner«, remarked Wotton, »and as he eats he converses with those about him.«[56] Whilst this was presumably only true for a given value of »anyone« (those with the entree to court, for instance, and thus probably of noble rank), it is still hard to imagine a bigger shift from Elizabeth's abstract formality, and this was undoubtedly deliberate.

54 *CSP Spain*, Vol. I, p. 387.

55 Levin (as note 27), pp. 80-81, see also 76. From John Lingard, *A History Of England From The First Invasion By The Romans*, 3rd ed., London 1825, Vol. 8, p. 587.

56 Quoted David Starkey et al, *The English Court from the Wars of the Roses to the Civil War*, Essex: Longman, 1987, p. 180.

Clothing, culture, control

Moreover, the privacy Elizabeth accorded actual food intake coincided over her reign with a new fashion which narrowed and lengthened already rigid bodices and narrowed waists. In 1577, Jerome Lippomano described the influential French fashion as consisting of

> inconceivably narrow waists; they [Frenchwomen] swell out their gowns from the waist downwards by whaleboned stuffs ... which increases the elegance of their figures. Over the chemise they wear a corset or bodice ... which makes their shape more delicate and slender ...[57]

Two decades later, a possessed girl was heard to demand from her demon a petticoat with

> a French bodie, not of whalebone, for that is not stiff enough, but of horne that will hold it out [...] to keep in my belly ...[58]

Clearly a fashionable and noble shape was associated with thinness, hence its desirability for a peasant girl dreaming of higher status. Whilst the famous portrait of Elizabeth as Princess shows her noticeably slender, over the course of her reign, perhaps unsurprisingly, she put on weight. By the 1580s, in her late forties and fifties, Janet Arnold's *Queen Elizabeth's Wardrobe Unlock'd* cites payments to tailors William Whittell and William Jones for the »alteringe enlargeing newe makeing & lininge of thirty peire of bodies ...«[59] Arnold states:

> The fashions of the first half of her reign were more flattering to the figure than the later styles; and the small waist, constricted body, widening sleeves and cone-shaped Spanish farthingale would have made Elizabeth appear even slimmer and taller than she was. The elaborate clothes worn during the later years of the reign create an impression of wealth and majesty. Although less flattering as it tended to cut the figure in half, and thus make it appear shorter, the wide drum-shaped farthingale, fashionable from the 1590s onwards, was certainly impressive and offered a larger area of skirt for ornamentation.

That »slimness« is paramount is not in doubt; moreover, the coincidence of wider skirts with the Queen's marginally increased girth to continue focus on a

57 Quoted Janet Arnold, *Queen Elizabeth's Wardrobe Unlock'd*, London: Maney Publishing, 1988, p. 147.

58 G. B. Harrison, *Elizabethan Journal*, quoted Arnold (as note 57), p. 146-147, via Edith Sitwell, *The Queens and the Hive*, Middlesex: Penguin, 1966, p. 471.

59 1585, Arnold (as note 57), p. 1; see also p. 2: between September 1587 and April 1589 102 enlargements were made.

proportionately narrow waist is also salient. Extensive use of patterning would have served to heighten this effect.

Whilst the »impressive« wider skirts did indeed offer more space for ideologically significant embroidered symbolism, Elizabeth's iconography of power derived not just from volume (as with Henrician fashion) but also from the deliberate and striking reduction in volume around the waist where contemporary line drawings of the female form emphasise a rounded belly.[60] Ironically, however, over her reign portraits became increasingly stylised, culminating in the Ditchley or Hardwick portraits with their strikingly elongated silhouettes and tiny waists. The more Elizabeth wanted to represent herself as an icon of power, the more attenuated her outline became, and the more focus was placed on a disproportionately slender waistline. A clear progression is evident from the naturalistic outlines of early portraits, when Elizabeth was actually thinner, to the increasingly artificial later ones. The implication is clear: for Elizabethan women, particularly the Queen herself, power is derived from control, rather than consumption, and its visual manifestation, with the aid of extensive corsetry and undergarmentage, paramount. Such fashions moved the female body away from the roundness and abundance expressed in anatomies and paintings as a »natural« female shape to emphasise an androgynous etiolation similar to that evident in the extended frontpieces of men's doublets.

If curves symbolise the visible, »natural« state of a femininity primarily associated with nature rather than culture, then to control them so rigorously not only represents the culturally imposed »virtue« presumed inherent in the constriction of natural appetites, but reinforces the association of curves with feminine weakness on whose metaphorical repudiation much of Elizabeth's rhetoric was based. That literal denial of appetite would serve to heighten the effect was simply a bonus. For the Queen in particular, the necessity of avoiding overconsumption, at the very least, in order to maintain such a silhouette, provided an additional reason to separate her eating from the public display of lavish abundance that still acted to demonstrate power. Moreover, hiding the actual transgression of the monarchal body's limits maintains the illusion of its impossibility, or at least the Queen's stringent control over it, in a manner perhaps akin to the contemporary anorexic's common refusal to eat before others – not only to hide the paucity of her actual food intake, but to maintain a façade of invulnerability. The modern

60 See, e. g., the Hardwick or Rainbow portraits of Elizabeth; Benjamin A. Rifkin, Michael J. Ackerman, *Human Anatomy: Depicting the Human Body from the Renaissance to Today*, London: Thames & Hudson, 2011; Jonathan Sawday, *The Body Emblazoned: Dissection and the Human Body in Renaissance Culture*, London: Routledge, 1996; J. Rueff, *De conceptu et gen. Hominis*, London 1580; Alexander Read, *Somatographia Anthropine, or a Description of the Body of Man*, London 1616. See also Arnold (as note 57).

anorexic, surrounded by abundance, perceives this invulnerability as broadcast by her steadfast resistance to the common human weakness of hunger, proclaiming both her individuality (as in her distinction from the norm) and her adequacy thereby. But the already unique and problematically distinct Elizabeth leaves the precise extent of her need as mysterious, deflecting curiosity onto lavish assertions of abundance. Paradoxically, the Queen's awkward gender enabled her to combine through the dining ritual not only the traditionally patriarchal display of power through infinite resource, but also a perversely feminine strength in the outward manifestation of consciously restricted food intake. In the context of contemporary truisms about appetite and femininity previously discussed, this heightened the androgyny and power of her public persona. To put it another way, whilst demonstrating the traditionally masculine control inherent in the possession and marshalling of abundant resources, the iconography she adopted and the restricted food intake it implied enabled her to demonstrate a self-control considerably greater in the context of her biological gender, and thus to reinforce her projected dominance. Whilst women's power is emphatically drawn from control rather than consumption, as Elizabeth's portraiture demonstrates, the concept of a masculinised »body politic« and the abstraction of her visible eating practices enabled her also to harness the symbolic power of ostentatiously rich and frequently exotic goods to considerable effect.

Susanne Scholz

»Dauncings true nobilitie«

Absent Queens in John Davies' *Orchestra* and Edmund Spenser's *The Faerie Queene* Book VI.

Elizabeth I's alleged passion for dancing looms large in the cultural imaginary of the twentieth and twenty-first centuries. Shekhar Kapur's feature film *Elizabeth* (1998), e. g., makes much of the queen's dances, especially with her favourite, the Earl of Leicester. These dances, however, are not historically verifiable. Although the queen liked to dance[1], dancing does not feature prominently as part of her political iconography (at least not during her own lifetime). On the contrary: her actual dancing may have been narrated on occasion, but it was not visualized as a spectacle of power. Traditionally, dance was seen as an enactment of cosmic harmony, and especially the dance of monarchs was conceived of as a medium to envision divine order for the eyes of the subjects. Dance, as a cultural practice which translates order into movement, always stages this order for an audience of spectators. The discussion of the queen's reticence concerning dance thus hinges on the question of what Elizabethan audiences would have seen while watching the queen dancing. While humanists had envisaged dance as a disciplinary discourse necessary for the fashioning of a good courtier, the increasing association of couple dancing with erotic desire interfered with the potential of dance to represent divine order and made it ultimately impossible to visualize the dance of the female monarch. Nevertheless, the royal dance is conjured up, if *ex negativo*, in the cultural productions of the time. In order to make this

I would like to thank Holly Crocker and Daniel Dornhofer for discussing earlier versions of this article with me.

1 Cf. the Scottish ambassador's account of 1563/64: »But I was stayed two days longer, till I might see her dance, as I was informed. Which being done, she enquired of me whether she or my queen danced best. I answered that the queen [Mary Queen of Scots, SSch.] danced not so high and disposedly as she did.« *The Memoirs of Sir James Melville of Halhill*, ed. by Gordon Donaldson, London 1969, p. 39. In later years, she was still fond of dancing but did apparently no longer dance herself, as the French ambassador de Maisse relates in 1597: »She takes great pleasure in dancing and music. She told me that she entertained at least sixty musicians; in her youth she danced very well, and composed measures and music, and had played them herself and danced them.« André Hurault, Sieur de Maisse, *A Journal of all that was Accomplished by Monsieur de Maisse, Ambassador in England from King Henry IV to Queen Elizabeth*, Anno Domini 1597, transl. from the French by G. B. Harrison and R. A. Jones, London 1931, p. 95.

point, this paper will contrast the dance in *The Faerie Queene*'s Book VI with another late Elizabethan instance of dance poetry, John Davies' *Orchestra* from 1596. Both imagine a queen dancing, but in both cases, she refuses to oblige, so that the vision remains a hope, a wish, a mere dream of cosmic harmony. Just like their prime reader, Elizabeth, the fictional queens of the poems deliberately stay outside the visual economy of desire that is enacted through dance. Their absence thus signals both the elusiveness of female power and the impossibility to represent the female ›body politic‹ in the traditional patterns available for the male royal body.

I. Making concord visible

Book VI of Edmund Spenser's *The Faerie Queene* culminates in a vision of the dance of the graces which is spied on by Calidore, the knight of courtesy. Set in a pastoral environment, this dance allegedly constitutes not only the climax of the quest for courtesy, but also »the most important allegorical core of the entire *The Faerie Queene*«.[2] This is a somewhat astonishing perception of that scene (shared by many Spenser scholars), given that none of the dancers participates in the quest, that it takes place in a location far from court and that even here, Gloriana remains invisible. What readers see, mediated by the raptured eye of Calidore, is »a troupe of Ladies [...] dauncing/ Full merrily, and making gladfull glee,/ And in the midst a Shepheard piping he did see.«[3] The bevy of maidens dancing in rounds to the lays of a not so unknown shepherd, Colin Clout, encircle and almost hide the centre of the allegorical vision, the three graces, complemented by a forth, unnamed country girl, who is apparently Colin Clout's sweetheart. When Calidore makes his presence known, however, the dancers vanish before he can make sense of what he sees.

It might not seem astonishing, at first, to find the graces engaged in a country dance. Dance as an image of concord occurs rather often as the closing image in Elizabethan pageants and plays. However, read against the background of some major changes in the discourse and practices of dancing in the early modern period, this pastoral dance in the book of courtesy raises some questions. For whose eyes is this dance staged? If this is a vision of (worldly) concord, why are no men involved in the dance? Why does it take place away from court? Is courtesy the

2 E. J. Bellamy, »The Faerie Queene (1596)«, in: R. A. McCabe (ed.), *The Oxford Handbook of Edmund Spenser,* Oxford 2010, p. 288. See also C. S. Lewis's, Kathleen Williams's and A. C. Hamilton's commentary in Edmund Spenser, *The Faerie Queene*, ed. by A. C. Hamilton, London and New York 1987, p. 689. All quotations from *The Faerie Queene* are from this edition.

3 *Faerie Queene* VI.x.10

epitome of concord or its antithesis? And most importantly, if it is an image of universal harmony, where is Gloriana? It is my contention that the dance of the graces in the pastoral idyll of Mount Acidale must be read against the practices of courtly dancing and especially the (imagined) dance of the queen, which also traditionally functions as an embodiment of concord and cosmic harmony. It will then appear that the absence of Gloriana from the scene is its most important statement – and one which runs counter to the fantasy of harmony that is allegedly the core of *The Faerie Queene*'s vision of order. If order can only be envisaged as patriarchal, these fantasies must ultimately be undermined by the presence of the queen. Her absence, on the other hand, may leave the fantasy intact, but display its phantasmatic nature. The imagined dance of the queen can then be read as a fantasy of subjugation of the female ruler under the kinetic codes which enforce a patriarchal and hierarchical social order. The fact that it does not take place thus highlights the queen's agency as well as the precarious nature of royal (self-)representation.

John Davies' *Orchestra*, probably written in 1594, at a time when he was still a student of law at the Middle Temple, foregrounds visions of order and harmony which he finds exemplified in courtly dancing. The poem, which appeared in print in 1596, the same year as Books IV to VI of *The Faerie Queene*, relates a conversation between chaste Penelope, still waiting for the return of her husband Odysseus, and Antinous, one of her suitors. Contrary to the story told by Homer, where Antinous is a treacherous suitor who is the first to be slain by Odysseus, Antinous appears as a model courtier who casts dance as the paradigm of ordered movement and thus establishes a system of metaphoric correspondences from the dance of the spheres via the dance of the elements and objects of nature down to the social order in a courtly world. He tries to persuade Penelope to dance by making her aware of its cosmic importance, showing her the different forms the dance can take in nature, its relevance for societies and even its manifestations in the ordered play of the parts of her own body, both in movement and speech.[4] Davies' argument taps into a number of classical texts, foremost among them Lucian's *Dialogue on the Dance*, but also Plato's *Timaeus* and the *Laws*, all of which had been made use of in humanist apologies of dancing such as Sir Thomas Elyot's *Book Named the Governor* (1531).

The early modern period witnessed major changes in the cultural practices and social codes of dancing which in turn reflected and negotiated changes in the structure of early modern societies. Skiles Howard summarizes: »As the Middle Ages waned, the dancing of the elite began a separate development, evolving

4 John Davies, *Orchestra or a Poeme of Dauncing Iudicially Proouing the True Obseruation of Time and Measure, in the Authenticall and Laudable Vse of Dauncing* (1596) STC 6360, st. 34-59, pp. 105-107.

into a means of courtly self-fashioning, an instrument for the acquisition and exercise of social power. [...] The dancing of the elite was a fully framed political discourse, an elaborate system of kinetic, spatial, and visual terms and interrelated ideas that organized a view of the world and the body that vindicated itself and excluded others.«[5] Howard shows how pictorial representations of dancers in the fifteenth and sixteenth centuries depict the bodies of noble and rustic dancers as belonging to different orders of society. The differentiation staged here casts the aristocratic couple, dancing in a stately and measured way, as the norm to be aspired to. She concludes that from the early modern period on, it is the aristocratic couple which comes to stand in for divine harmony.[6] Sir Thomas Elyot's *Governor*, for instance, makes much of the image of the gendered couple as a model for human concord and sees dance as a way of representing the perfection of creation and of human relationships:

> In every dance, of a most ancient custom, there danceth together a man and a woman, holding each other by the hand or the arm, which betokeneth concord. Now it behoveth the dancers and also the beholders of them to know all qualities incident to a man, and also all qualities to a woman likewise appertaining. A man in his natural perfection is fierce, hardy, strong in opinion, covetous of glory, desirous of knowledge, appetiting by generation to bring forth his semblable. The good nature of a woman is to be mild, timorous, tractable, benign, of sure remembrance, and shamefast. [...] Wherefore, when we behold a man and a woman dancing together, let us suppose there to be a concord of all the said qualities [...]. These qualities, in this wise being knit together and signified in the personages of man and woman dancing, do express or set out the figure of very nobility.[7]

Elyot's tract envisions an ideal of gender complementarity which reflects the perfection of the first creation and which hinges on the partners' compliancy in fulfilling the respective behaviour norms. In tune with the overall disciplinary gist of his text, he sees dance as a way of representing the ideal of a well-fashioned courtly body for an implied audience of spectators.

Thoinot Arbeau, in one of the most influential dancing tracts of the time, the *Orchésographie* of 1588, also points to the civilizing capacities of dancing, and he goes beyond the mere metaphorical use of moving in harmony to the more practical aspects of how to choose a spouse:

5 Skiles Howard, *The Politics of Courtly Dancing*, Amherst 1998, pp. 3 and 23.

6 Ibid., esp. pp. 1-45 and 69-92.

7 Thomas Elyot, *The Book Named the Governor*, ed. by S. E. Lehmberg, London 1966, I.xxi., pp. 77-78.

> You have taken the proper view, because it is only natural that the male and female should seek each other, and nothing more disposes a man to acts of courtesy, honour and generosity than love; and, if you desire to marry, you should know that a mistress is won by the pleasant disposition and grace with which one is observed to dance [...]. There is more even in it than this, for dancing is practised to make manifest whether lovers are in good health and sound in all their limbs, after which it is permitted to them to kiss their mistresses, whereby they may perceive if either has an unpleasant breath or exhales a disagreeable odour as that of bad meat: so that, in addition to divers other merits attendant on dancing, it has become essential for the well-being of society.[8]

This is the cosmic potential and also the crux of dancing, because in the context of match making, the meeting of the sexes in dance also entails dangers, as opponents of the dance, especially from Puritan quarters, never get tired to point out:

> Dancing is the vilest vice of all and truly it cannot be easily said what mischiefs the sight, and the hearing do receive hereby, which afterward be the cause of communication and embracing. They dance with disordinate gestures, and with monstrous thumping of the feet, to pleasant sounds, to wanton songs, to dishonest verses. Maidens and matrons are groped and handled with unchaste hands, and kissed, and dishonestly embraced: and the things which nature hath hidden, modestly covered, are then often-time by means of lasciviousness, made naked, and ribaldry, under the colour of pastime is dissembled.[9]

Couple dancing obviously needs to be policed rigidly and it entails a strictly hierarchical ordering of the dancers in terms of rank and, of course, gender. It tacitly implies a subjection of the female partner under the lead of the male and thus, on a symbolic plane, a naturalization of a patriarchal order. As the examples make clear, dance can be seen as a kinetic code which translates social and gender hierarchy into (more or less natural) movement. As a performance of order, it needs both competent performers and spectators who judge the success of the performance. This is also why Arbeau and other dancing masters permanently admonish their pupils to control their bodies:

8 Thoinot Arbeau, *Orchésography. A Treatise in the Form of a Dialogue. Whereby all Manner of Persons my Easily Acquire and Practice the Honourable Exercise of Dancing,* transl. from the original ed. published at Langres 1588 by Cyril W. Beaumont, New York 1965, p. 18.

9 John Northbrooke, *A Treatise Against Dicing, Dancing, Plays and Interludes* (1577), London 1843, p. 136.

> [W]hen you dance in company never look down to examine your steps and ascertain if you dance them correctly. Hold your head and body upright with a confident mien, and do not spit or blow your nose much. And if necessity obliges you to do so, turn your head away and use a fair white handkerchief. Converse pleasantly in a low and modest voice, let your arms fall by your side neither in a lifeless nor in a restless manner, and be suitably and neatly dressed, your hose well drawn up and your shoes clean.[10]

All humanists writing in favour of dancing emphasized the capacity of dance to civilize the untutored body and refine it into an instrument of courtly identity. Seen in this vein, dance is one of the prime examples for the precarious balance of sincerity and superficiality that is so characteristic for early modern courtly discourse: if it disciplines the naturally ›grotesque‹ body, it also places much emphasis on appearances and shiny surfaces. Just like the linguistic codes of courtly speech, the kinetic codes of courtliness must be acquired in order to equip the courtier with the necessary gracefulness or *sprezzatura*. Both modes of articulating the courtly self, however, labour under the paradox of exemplifying higher truths by outside show, by inextricably intertwining the natural and the artificial. Graceful movement must become ›second nature‹ to the courtier and the dancer, while the graceful ›movement‹ of words is an indispensable precondition of finding favour at court. Dance is thus part of the discourse of courtly self-fashioning, and just like the well-measured use of words, it has the potential for transcendence.

This transcendent moment, the capacity of dance to represent or even embody higher truths, is especially relevant in relation to the monarch's dance. Generally, humanist culture had envisioned dancing as a way of understanding »the truth of the cosmos and therefore the nature of God«.[11] Unsurprisingly, then, the representative of God on earth was thought capable of envisioning this harmony to beholders from less perfect ranks, to make them learn what perfection is and try to emulate it by disciplining their bodies in the same way. Mark Franko and others have alerted us to the eminently symbolic function of the monarch's dance, which embodies (rather than represents) divine harmony and which makes it visible to his/ her subjects.[12] This view of dance as a transcendent practice has its origin in Platonic notions of the cosmic dance of the spheres and planets at the

10 Arbeau (as note 8), p. 103.

11 Jennifer Nevile, *The Eloquent Body. Dance and Humanist Culture in Fifteenth-Century Italy*, Bloomington and Indianapolis 2004, p. 104.

12 Cf. Mark Franko, *Dance as Text. Ideologies of the Baroque Body*, Cambridge 1993, and »Figural Inversions of Louis XIV's Dancing Body«, in: Mark Franko and Annette Richards (eds.), *Acting on the Past. Historical Performance Across the Disciplines*, Hanover and London 2000, pp. 35-51.

beginning of the world (*Timaeus* 40a-d and *Laws* II, 653e-657b).[13] Its Renaissance re-launch is especially suggestive when seen in the light of the political fiction of the two bodies of the sovereign. Many scholars have argued that the hyperbolic representations of Elizabeth as never-aging, ever beautiful virgin queen stage the fiction of the political body which is subject neither to age nor infirmity, thereby disseminating a concept which was originally re-vamped in order to deal with the pressing problem of the succession of an unmarried queen.[14] Ideally, the (imagined) spectacle of the dancing queen could be understood as another articulation of this ›political theology‹, a dance of the body politic[15], by which the queen partakes in the divine order of the cosmos. In his/ her political body, the monarch permanently performs a spectacle of divine and worldly power. The royal body thus functions as an instrument of moral instruction and must be *seen* by its subjects, not only in order for them to learn their place in the ›microcosmic‹ constellation of the court, but also because the divine aura of the royal body ›re-charges‹ itself by being looked at.[16] And just as it is the subjects' duty to acknowledge the power of the sovereign (if by gazing and gawping), it is the monarch's duty to make divine order visible, and this is why the speaker of John Davies' poem exhorts princes to learn to dance:

> Learne then to daunce you that are Princes borne
> And lawfull lords of earthly creatures all;
> [...]
> And imitate the starres caelestiall.[17]

II. Spectacles of power

This practice of envisioning kingship emphasizes the privileged visibility of the monarch. At the time, being at the centre of visual interest was not yet a sign of objectification but a token of divine legitimation and the capacity to embody

13 Cf. James Miller, *The Measure of Wisdom. The Cosmic Dance in Classical and Christian Antiquity*, Toronto et al 1986.

14 Cf., among others, Roy Strong, *The Cult of Elizabeth. Elizabethan Portraiture and Pageantry*, London 1977, and *Gloriana. The Portraits of Queen Elizabeth I.*, London 1987. See also my *Body Narratives. Writing the Nation and Fashioning the Subject in Early Modern England*, Basingstoke 2000, for a more detailed explanation of the nexus, in the cult of Elizabeth, of temporal continuity and spatial representation.

15 Marie Axton, *The Queen's Two Bodies*, London 1977, p. 12. The *locus classicus* dealing with the concept is of course Ernst Kantorowicz, *The King's Two Bodies*, Princeton 1957.

16 Franko, »Figural Inversions« (as note 12), p. 44.

17 *Orchestra* (as note 4), st. 60.

higher truths. The interaction between sovereign and subjects thus described draws heavily on issues of vision and visuality, of seeing and being seen. Since the court must also be understood as a visual arrangement catering to many eyes/ ›I‹s, this interaction has a collective dimension: In watching the sovereign, subjects form a community of spectators which experiences a moment of divine grace by watching the graceful movements of their sovereign. Attention, as Janette Dillon has pointed out, drawing on Jonathan Crary's notion of suspension, can imply a suspended temporality, a moment out of time in which the raptured gaze absorbs truths from another plane.[18] This attention is more than a visual epiphany, it is also a bodily experience. Attention is of course a currency at the early modern court: courtiers and ladies needed to be seen by the queen in order to acquire and ascertain their place. Inversely, the queen's performance of power must be seen by the subjects in order to take effect. Such a moment of joint elevation, of shared rapture accompanied by a shared emotional investment can function as a solidifying element in a community and establish a feeling of belonging which at the same time creates a collective as it confirms the order on which it stands.[19] And even if courtly performance constitutes an elite entertainment, royal entries and progresses also drew beholders from lower strata of society. For the witnesses of the spectacle, this joint elation is not only a visual experience; it involves the body in space. It is about expectant tension, about positioning oneself vis-à-vis the queen, about knowing one's place and timing one's performance. All this could paradigmatically apply to the dancing of the queen, yet we have little evidence that Elizabeth used this medium of putting her power on display.

So I am not claiming here that Elizabethan courtiers actually ever experienced such a moment of elevation when they saw their queen dancing. We know from French court entertainments that the young Louis XIV staged himself in this way, yet evidence from Elizabeth's court is sparse when it comes to the queen's dances. Coronation and other royal entries, however, carefully staged moments of intense attention, almost adoration of the queen; so obviously, the visual experience of awed gazing with its concomitant suspension of temporality was not completely unknown to Elizabethan subjects.[20]

On Mount Acidale, Calidore's experience of the graces' dance becomes just such a moment of intense visual adoration and it can be assumed that the object of his gazing is a displaced version of the queen. Yet Calidore is alone in his raptured state, and when he later shares his experience with Colin, the moment

18 Janette Dillon, *The Language of Space in Court Performance, 1400 – 1625*, Cambridge 2010, p. 15. She draws on Jonathan Crary, *Suspensions of Perception: Attention, Spectacle, and Modern Culture*, Cambridge, MA and London 2000, p. 10.

19 Dillon (as note 18), pp. 20-21.

20 Ibid.

itself is over. Moreover, while gazing on the dance, he experiences first and foremost an awareness that it is not for his eyes to see:

He durst not enter into th'open greene
For dread of them vnwares to be descryde,
For breaking of their daunce, if he were seene;
But in the couert of the wood did byde,
Beholding all, yet of them unespyde.
There he did see, that pleased much his sight,
That euen he him selfe his eyes enuyde,
An hundred naked maydens lilly white,
All raunged in a ring, and dauncing in delight.

All they without were raunged in a ring,
All danced round; but in the midst of them
Three other Ladies did both daunce and sing,
The whilest the rest them round about did hemme,
And like a girlond did in compasse stemme:
And in the midst of those same three, was placed
Another Damzell, as precious gemme,
Amidst a ring most richly well enchaced,
That with her goodly presence all the rest much graced.[21]

The poem invests some energy to stress the fact that this is a round dance, performed by women only, for their own pleasure and delight, but also, one could suspect, for the instruction of the viewer and, by implication, the reader. A closer look at the history of dance in pre-modern times shows that round dances traditionally centred on a figure of power, while the circle itself symbolized not only the perfect form but also the perennial renewal of the powers of life.[22] Davies' *Orchestra* casts the round dance as a figure of ›primeval‹ order in which planets, elements and objects of nature dance and into which the God of Love forces the archaic hoards of uncivilized humans in order to ›tame‹ them. Dancing in circles is a means of appropriating space, and it clearly has a collective aspect,

21 *Faerie Queene* VI.x.11-12.

22 In his seminal *The World History of the Dance* (1937, German orig. 1933) Curt Sachs speaks of ancient practices in which the round dance was performed, for example at burials and during Shrovetide. He claims that enclosing an object such as a totem or a maypole means appropriating, even incorporating the object or its powers. Curt Sachs, *The World History of the Dance*, New York 1963, pp. 114 and 100. In their late medieval variety, round dances frequently took place in a religious context such as the annunciation or nativity. Later, Howard claims, they were associated with fairies and witches, and eventually denigrated as a lower class practice. Howard (as note 5), p. 8.

with the holding of hands and linking of arms implying a unity of movement and direction. Round dancing thus establishes and represents community (Davies even draws a parallel to exercising troops).[23] Even beyond the consolidation of social rank and hierarchy which seems to be Davies' foremost occupation, it introduces a more inclusive vision of community, »where gentle and common interact«.[24] With the emergence of courtly dancing as the model practice, dancing in rounds gradually came to be considered as a rural, if not rustic, kind of entertainment.[25] But despite their outmodedness as a medium of articulating a courtly self, round dances still featured prominently in progresses and other entertainments for the queen. In a pastoral context, it seems, circle dances could still stand as a (maybe nostalgic, or completely phantasmatic) image for the perfectly harmonious community.[26]

However, even a cursory glance at what Calidore sees on Mount Acidale shows that this dance does not symbolize collective concord on a ›national‹ scale. Whereas Davies presents an idealist vision of a dance of »diuers men and women [...]/ Obseruing perfect uniformitie:/ All turne together, all together trace,/ And all together honor and embrace«[27], no men join the dance on Mount Acidale, so it does not easily suggest itself as an image of national community. What Davies describes is a *basse danse* or measures, a processional dance of (mostly gendered) couples which, because it joins old and young, men and women, and possibly also higher and lower ranks, can function as an image of national unity. What Calidore witnesses, by contrast, is a circle of naked maidens dancing around the three graces, a somehow otherworldly vision. Clearly, in terms of its symbolic potential, this is a different kind of dance.

III. Containing tension

It seems that the literature of the time used the discourse of dancing with its internal contradictions in order to negotiate desires and anxieties about the status not only of the subject's bodies (in need of refinement), but also of the royal body.

23 *Orchestra* (as note 4), st. 87. On this analogy see also William H. McNeill, *Keeping Together in Time. Dance and Drill in Human History*, Cambridge, MA 1995. Cf. Mark Franko, *Dance as Text* (as note 12), pp. 30-31, on the subjection of bodies in geometrical dance.

24 Howard (as note 5), p. 73.

25 Ibid., esp. pp. 69-92.

26 Cf. also Puttenham's poems »A general Resemblance of the Roundell to God, the World, and the Queene« and »A special and particular resemblance of her Maiestie to the Roundell« in: George Puttenham, *The Arte of English Poesie*, ed. by G. D. Willcock and A. Walker, Cambridge 1970, pp. 98-100.

27 *Orchestra* (as note 4), st. 110.

The political body of the monarch, as we know from Kantorowicz, is not only beyond the shortcomings and ailments of the natural body, it is also ungendered. This is an important point which may help to clarify why the dance in gendered couples – and with it the queen dancing as the female partner of a couple – is such a precarious image. The confirmation, acceptance and re-iteration of the social order through dancing, I have argued so far, is always celebrated for an audience of spectators. Yet, given the ambivalence of dancing in heterosexual couples, what happens if beholders see the queen, in courtly entertainment as well as in the context of marriage negotiations, as part of a gendered couple? While subjecting her to a kinetic code which tacitly acknowledges the superiority of the male partner, couple dance also implicitly sexualizes her body, directing the gaze away from her ›body politic‹ towards her ›body natural‹. If this way of perceiving the queen becomes the dominant perspective, a notion of embodiment (in the quasi-sacramental sense of ›full presence‹) of the political body gradually becomes impossible.

Davies' originality, as Sarah Thesiger claims, lies in the way he introduces a great God of Love as the originator both of the world, the social order of its denizens, and dance. While love is the ordering principle and creative force of the universe, dance emerges as a way of bodying forth this creative power[28], whether in the form of the harmony of the elements in nature or as a way of ordering social relations in a harmonic (i. e. hierarchical) way. Finally, at the microcosmic end of the chain, the court can also be understood as an ordered cosmos, with the planets and fixed stars revolving around the central lodestar, the queen.

Davies' articulations of harmonious movement, be it of elements of nature, be it of social actors at (Penelope's) court, are clearly more mundane than Spenser's. In his view, the court is an enactment of order which dance articulates and teaches. Davies clearly speaks about aristocratic couples dancing and so representing order in variety, and when he presents a reversal of gender order this only serves to make the final image of ›natural‹ harmony even more convincing:

> What if by often interchange of place
> Sometime the woman gets the upper hand?
> That is but done for more delightful grace,
> For on that part she doth not ever stand;
> But, as the measure's law doth her command,
> She wheels about and ere the dance doth end
> Into her former place she doth transcend.[29]

28 Sarah Thesiger, »The Orchestra of Sir John Davies and the Image of the Dance«, in: *Journal of the Warburg and Courtauld Institutes* 36 (1973), pp. 277-304, here p. 290.

29 *Orchestra* (as note 4), st. 112.

The harmony envisioned here hinges on the compliance of the queen, because she is at the same time the true embodiment and heavenly guarantor of concord, being addressed as »faire soule which came from heau'n aboue,/ To rule thys house, another heau'n below.«[30] It is a queen's duty to translate the metaphysical idea of concord into the social milieu of those she rules, in the hope that this will have a civilizing effect. Here again dance is advocated by Antinous, the poem's prime speaker, as the suitable medium; after having explained the ordering impact that love has on all creatures in nature, he concludes:

Loe this is Dauncings true nobilitie.
Dauncing the child of Musick and of Loue,
Dauncing it selfe both loue and harmony,
VVhere all agree, and all in order moue;
Dauncing the Art that all Arts doe approue:
The faire Caracter of the worlds consent,
The heau'ns true figure, and th'earths ornament.[31]

Skiles Howard argues that Davies' poem »mythologizes [dance] as the transcendent organizing practice of civic life.«[32] In its progression from the dance of the elements to the ordering of the »disordered rout«[33] by casting them into a ring or hay, to the ultimate vision of perfection in courtly dance, the poem dramatizes a process of civilization which should eventually, so Antinous desires, culminate in Penelope's dance.

Being the epitome of the chaste woman, the figure of Penelope herself could be seen as a tribute to Queen Elizabeth, the implicit addressee of Davies' poem.[34] Yet on another level, the English court is introduced into the poem as a paradigmatic ordered space, when Penelope gazes into a magic mirror which shows her

The fairest sight that euer shall be seene,
And th'onely wonder of posteritie,
The richest worke in Natures treasury;
Which she disdaines to shew on this worlds stage,
And thinks it far too good for our rude age.

But in another world deuided far,
In the great, fortunate, triangled Ile,
Thrise twelue degrees remou'd from the North star

30 Ibid., st. 108.
31 Ibid., st. 96.
32 Howard (as note 5), p. 61.
33 *Orchestra* (as note 4), st. 29.
34 The poem itself was dedicated to Davies' friend Richard Martin.

Shee will this glorious workmanship compile
Which shee hath been conceiuing all thys while
Since the worlds birth, & will bring forth at last,
When sixe and twenty hundreth yeeres are past.[35]

Making use of the typical double time structure of national narratives, construing a past while drafting norms and ideals to be reached in the future, the poem here casts the ordered English court as the telos of history seen in a vision by Penelope, whose own court is far from that ordered state. It links notions of cosmic harmony, the dance of the spheres and the order of Elizabeth's court. While this is to be expected in a panegyric poem of a flatterer like Davies (whose »Hymns to Astraea« which appeared three years later hyperbolically praised the queen), the total absence of Elizabeth from Penelope's vision is astonishing. The obvious next step in Davies' argument should have been to compare the two queens, but he refrains from doing so and the poem's original version ends rather lamely with an invocation of the muses to help represent »this great worke diuine«.[36] Tillyard claims that the poem is unfinished and that Davies planned to represent in detail what he only alludes to: the »glorious English courts diuine Image«.[37] This is by no means certain; pace Tillyard, Elizabeth remains all but absent from the poem's original version. Tillyard's own edition from 1948 adds stanzas 132-37 from the edition of Davies' *Nosce Teipsum* of 1622, to which Orchestra was appended. These four stanzas provide a representation of the queen, but they were probably written after her death. Yet also in the extended version, it is only her courtiers who dance:

For of her barons brave and ladies fair
(Who had they been elsewhere most fair had been)
Many an incomparable lovely pair
With hand in hand were interlinked seen,
Making fair honour to their sovereign queen.
Forward they pac'd and did their pace apply
To a most sweet and solemn melody.[38]

35 *Orchestra* (as note 4), st. 120-21.

36 Ibid., st. 129.

37 Ibid., st. 126. Sir John Davies, *Orchestra, or: A Poem of Dancing*, ed. with intro by E. M. W. Tillyard, London 1945, p. 13. Tillyard also devotes a chapter to the cosmic dance and Davies' poem in his influential *The Elizabethan World Picture*, Harmondsworth 1970, orig. Chatto & Windus 1943, pp. 123-129. It seems symptomatic that Tillyard re-launches this fantasy of order in a time of severe cultural stress; the »perilously poised world« (p. 129) he attributes to the contemporaries of Elizabeth is clearly also his own.

38 *Orchestra* (as note 4), st. 133.

Even this vision, which Penelope beholds »rapt with sweet pleasure«[39], does not incite her to dance. But is this really due to prejudice and stubbornness on her part, as Tillyard seems to suggest? Given Antinous' reputation in the *Odyssee*, we must be wary of the reliability of his narrative. On the one hand, he closely follows Lucian and his humanist readers in representing dance as an image of both natural and social order. But on the other hand, his goal is ultimately to win Penelope for himself – to be »the mouer [...] to turne about/ Those glorious ornaments that Youth and Loue/ have fixed in you [i. e. Penelope]«[40] – and his narrative is inflected with this desire. Antinous' mistake, or maybe his treacherousness, lies in pressing Penelope to dance in courtly fashion – and ideally with him – while she should be the figure of admiration and adoration at the centre of a round dance. In other words, he confuses the work of love – the cosmic dance of elements which can only be represented in a dance which re-iterates the perfect form: the circle – with the work of desire which lies behind the social dances taking place in the eroticized climate of the court. At court, personal interests interfere with political considerations and hierarchies are no longer natural but must be negotiated – among other things via dance practices and the proximity of the single courtier/ dancer to the queen. When Penelope projects her vision of courtly dancing far into the future, she imaginatively leaves Antinous and the other selfish suitors behind, dreaming herself into a more perfect time and space in which, so the argument seems to imply, the queen might be allowed to dance in the suitable fashion because she is at the centre of a ›natural‹ order.

Considering the suggested analogy between Penelope and Queen Elizabeth, another question arises: why Penelope? The analogy is not obvious, nor is it conventional: there are no other Penelope-comparisons to represent the queen in Elizabethan literature. Penelope is a married woman trying to rule a household from which her husband is absent. As we know from Homer, there is no order at her court: her suitors infringe on Odysseus' lawful position and do not respect her or her son Telemachos' right to rule the household at Ithaca; there is no real figure of authority present. This is a court in disorder, and part of the havoc is ascribed to Penelope's refusal to choose a new husband. Here, parallels between Penelope and Elizabeth seem to open up, but they are neither flattering nor historically fitting: when Davies wrote his poem, time for choice was over and Elizabeth had long (been) turned into the ›Virgin Queen‹. However, a closer look at Penelope's reaction to Antinous' barely veiled desire shows that she probably understands better than he does what the vision is all about. Antinous represents the great God of Love as the driving force behind all movement in the cosmos, yet it is by no means clear that the order which he praises follows naturally.

39 Ibid., st. 134.
40 Ibid., st. 13.

On the contrary: order may well be the *project* that lies behind the necessity to form into a ›dance‹, a way of disciplining the potentially chaotic forces in the universe. Dance thus emerges as the ordered form of the energy this god invests creation with. The emphasis is here on the necessity of civilizing action: only if the elements, forces of nature, and human denizens of the world are reconfigured into ›dancers‹ can they embody divine order. The suitors at Penelope's court, however, are still in a ›state of nature‹, pursuing their unbridled desires which are only held in check by homosocial competition, not yet by the civilizing force of love. So this is the task which Penelope cannot yet fulfil and which sets the agenda for Elizabeth's ›Golden Age‹. In the historical progression this prophetic vision implies, men must undergo a process of civilization and refine and polish themselves. If this is what the dance is about, Antinous is mistaken (or actively misleading) when he pressurizes Penelope to choose him as a partner in her dance. Clearly, the vision does not promise choice of a husband, on the contrary: harmony seems out of the question when the queen prefers one man over the rest. And far from changing this general tenor of the argument, the 1622 addition to the poem rather envisages a Petrarchist model of all courtiers doing homage to their queen. Elizabeth is here at the centre of the courtly dance, but she does not dance herself.

In denying the dance, Penelope makes the point (well-worn in Elizabethan panegyrics) that the queen cannot belong to one man only, and while she is not generally opposed to dance as an image of order, her proper dancing mode would be the circle, which unites disparate elements into a meaningful collective. Since this is barred through the selfish desires of her suitors, there is no way out for her but dreaming of future harmony and refusing to oblige in the present. Given the underlying sexual tension at Penelope's court at Ithaca, her dancing would probably even worsen the situation, unleash the aggressive ›individualism‹ of the suitors and maybe destroy the court completely. All the negative effects of dance would come to the fore, as she herself points out, claiming that dancing fosters »vainnesse, frenzie, and misorder«.[41] Penelope's response, in which she quotes mythological instances of lust-driven dancers wreaking havoc on their respective societies, seems to take the stand of Puritan dance-haters, yet the motivation behind it derives from more than merely qualms about sexual morality.

So in Penelope's wise decision to ignore Antinous' pressing demands, the poem foregrounds one of the predicaments of the discourse of dancing, i. e. the individuation and sexualisation of the partners. Even if Antinous is a good suitor, his gaze is desirous and sexually charged. To dance with him would be to yield – to his powers of persuasion and ultimately to his sexual wishes. So

41 Ibid., st. 100.

although dance generally nobilitates the body, the dance of the queen's natural body cannot represent divine concord. As long as men pursue their own interests, the dancing queen is an impossible image.

IV. Coming full circle

Now, the juxtaposition of Penelope's and Elizabeth's courts at the end of Davies' poem suggests that Penelope is right to refuse to dance and that Elizabeth's absence from the original version of the poem suggests just as much: that the sacramental power of the queen's political body is undermined by the eroticization that comes with a couple dance. How does this resonate with the dance of the graces on Mount Acidale? Calidore's scopic position when he witnesses the dance of the graces is very similar to that of Penelope when she looks into the magic mirror. Both experience a moment of otherworldly perfection, both are taken out of their historical moment and suspend time and space and in the end both need a poet to explain to them what they have seen:

> Much wondred Calidore at this straunge sight,
> Whose like before his eye had neuer seene,
> And standing long astonished in spright,
> And rapt with pleasaunce, wist not what to weene;
> Whether it were the traine of beauties Queene,
> Or Nymphes, or Faeries, or enchanted show,
> With which his eyes mote haue deluded beene.
> Therefore resoluing, what it was, to know,
> Out of the wood he rose, and toward them did go.
>
> But soone as he appeared to their vew,
> They vanish't all away out of his sight.[42]

The position of »beholding all, yet [remaining] unespyde«[43] is one of power in the scopic regimes of modernity.[44] In the early modern period, it is still something of a ›godlike‹ position, and it could be argued that this constitutes Gloriana's

42 *Faerie Queene*, VI.x.17-18.
43 Ibid., VI.x.11.
44 Cf., among others, Jonathan Crary, *Techniques of the Observer*, Cambridge, MA and London 2001/1991, pp. 1-66.

perspective on the world of (and Elizabeth's on the text of) *The Faerie Queene*.[45] To assume this viewing point constitutes a transgression as well as an empowerment on the part of the perceiving subject, individualizing him or her from his surroundings. So unsurprisingly, Calidore, while watching, is painfully aware of his own unworthiness of seeing what he sees. Wonder, amazement and rapture, which are detailed as Calidore's feelings at the time, cast this as a Neoplatonic moment of visual elevation which is triggered by a vision of earthly beauty and which affords him a glimpse of heavenly beauty. Indeed, in the internal ›grammar‹ of the Faerie Queene, the dance occupies the position that projections of perfection and fulfilment usually assume: canto ten of almost every book provides its hero with a vision of the prospective fulfilment of the quest. So the dance, although its protagonists vanish when he stirs, may well be originally intended for Calidore's eyes, whose crouching position and feeling of unworthiness must then be understood as the suitable receptive condition for humans favoured with such visions.

Yet Calidore is not the only one to witness the graces. Colin Clout, Spenser's persona of the pastoral poet, is also allowed the visual experience which takes Calidore so much out of himself. What is more, by providing the music, he has a part in it himself. When the somnambulistic Calidore appears on the scene and dissipates the spectacle of grace, Colin breaks his pipes in despair. In the ensuing conversation between Calidore and Colin, the ignorant knight learns that the graces are courtesy in perfection, a state which is represented, so the poet claims, by the nakedness of the damsels, who appear in their ›natural perfection‹, as they never could at court, »without guile/ or false dissemblaunce«.[46] Seen in the general context of court critique, the central allegory of the book of courtesy implicitly pits pastoral versus courtly dance, drawing on the frequent analogies construed by humanists between the verses' feet and the dancer's feet, both in need of refinement and discipline in order to articulate a courtly self. We can assume that Calidore, who »by euery deede and worde that he did say [...] through both the eyes/ And both the eares did steale the heart away«[47] is also an accomplished dancer. So if dance features as a paradigmatic practice of courtesy, it balances both the promise of concord and the danger of manipulation. Pastoral and pastoral dance on the other hand, both in their aesthetic form (the circle) and their personnel (naked maidens) suggest closeness to ›natural‹ (i. e. ›unmanipulated‹) forms. As the reference to Ariadne's crown implies, the

45 Cf. Lisa Dickson, »The Prince of Rays: Spectacular Invisibility in Spenser's *The Faerie Queene*«, in: *Early Modern Literary Studies* 12 (2006), pp. 1-31, here p. 7; <http://purl.oclc.org/emls/12-2/dickprin.htm> (accessed March 2013).

46 *Faerie Queene* VI.x.24.

47 Ibid. VI.ii.3.

dance is also associated with cosmic constellations. Gloriana, however, who by the logic of circle dances should be at its centre, is nowhere to be seen. Spenser's pastoral version of the dance of the graces draws on the transcendental potential of the round dance, but significantly leaves out (or displaces) the centre. For even if Spenser uses pastoral dance as a deliberate archaism to envision the body politic (and thus also to provide a pattern for national unity), this perfect vision of harmony should have included Gloriana as the centre of power and prime embodiment of cosmic unity. So Gloriana's absence from the scene does not simply drive home the point that pastoral dancing has lost its capacity to embody divine concord; it highlights that even in this nostalgic vision of a perfect world, the queen is missing. Arcadian perfection in *The Faerie Queene* is not only impossible because there is, ultimately, no difference between courtly and pastoral worlds, it is also impossible because the queen does not submit to Spenser's patriarchal fantasy of order. Instead, she hovers over the scene as a non-material spectre, a disembodied gaze which sees all, yet remains unseen.

To conclude, Gloriana's absence, just like Penelope's refusal to dance in Davies' *Orchestra*, signals the impossibility of representing the ›cosmic‹ potential of the body politic in a practice that is increasingly predicated on an eroticizing gaze. By containing the potential for transcendence as well as the naturalisation of gender hierarchies, the discourse of dance negotiates the ambivalences both of the concept of the queen's two bodies and of emerging forms of subjectivity characterized by individuation and a stronger emphasis on the gendered body. Instead of having their bodies gazed at, disciplined and eroticized in dance, the queens in these poems, and by implication the historical queen who is their prime reader, stay outside the visual field, »beholding all, yet of them unespyde«.

Jackie Watson

»He writes, he railes, he jests, he courts, what not, / And all from out his huge long scraped stock / Of well penn'd playes«

Learning the Performance of Courtiership at the Early Modern Inns of Court

Described famously as the »third university«[1], and often attended after some years of more general education at Oxford or Cambridge, the four Inns of Court in London (Inner and Middle Temple, Lincoln's Inn and Gray's Inn) were officially centres to train young men in the law. However, their role in the early modern period was also, to some extent, as ›finishing schools‹, teaching young men the wider skills they would need to thrive in their future lives, and this article aims to address the question of how far the Inns prepared those men who were ambitious for future roles on the Elizabethan and Jacobean courtly stage. Working with primary material written by Innsmen themselves about their lives and activities, the records of revels such as the Middle Temple's *Prince D'Amour*, and manuals written to guide a largely Inns of Court readership, I shall argue that much of their training was quite consciously a process of encouraging conformity to a perceived ideal of courtly performance, and, further, that this training was recognized to be essentially dramatic. The process was predicated upon the idea of an influential spectator; the performance of courtiership and the meeting of the court's visual or verbal expectations were to secure the approval and acceptance of those men already there. Relevant here is Bourdieu's work on social positioning[2], and in this light, I argue that the cultural capital of the Inns as an institution enabled the young men who studied there to engage in the necessary ›self-fashioning‹ to secure preferment. Much scholarly attention has focused on the Inns' cultural role in early modern London, and their cultural proximity to the royal court, and the contribution to the field of a recent volume of essays edited by Jane Archer, Elisabeth Goldring and Sarah Knight is invaluable in demonstrating the

1 For example by George Buc[k], *The third universitie of England. Or a treatise of the foundations of all the colledges, auncient schooles of priviledge, and of houses of learning, and liberall arts, within and above the most famous cittie of London*, London 1615.

2 Pierre Bourdieu, *Ce que parler veut dire: l'économie des échanges linguistiques*, trans. Gino Raymond and Matthew Adamson, ed. John B Thompson, as *Language and Symbolic Power*, Cambridge 1991.

powerful influence the Inns had.[3] This cultural bond between the two centres of power – royal and legal – echoes a physical proximity, with both Inns and court on the western edge of life in the city and joining together in events such as revels, masques and plays which both entertained and represented the elite. Yet, this proximity can also conceal a more subversive quality to the Inns. Increasingly a source of opposition to the Jacobean royal prerogative, and highly conscious of the courtly performances in which they were being rehearsed, this article will finally explore satirical depictions of such courtly actors and their legal student understudies which reveal the process, and the tensions, behind this training. Hence I shall examine the context of the early modern Inns, and how they trained aspirant young men to conform, before I move on to the particular role played by the Inns of Court revels in this training, and finally explore how participation in the revels can be seen to demonstrate a curiously complex relationship between Inns, court and early modern drama.

It can be a scholarly pitfall to characterize an Inns of Court milieu as if it were a homogeneous construct with the same effect on all members. In fact, one must remember that it is not one unit, but four Inns, and entrance books reveal that each had a different social, and to some extent geographical, constitution at different points in its history. Within each Inn, members were not drawn from the same backgrounds and were in residence for widely differing reasons; keen students determined on a legal career jostled with rich young noblemen, country gentlemen gaining a London polish, and ambitious men of the middling sort who desired courtly preferment. Thus in this article, I focus primarily on men from the Middle Temple, much of the evidence I explore most closely comes from the 1590s and I am mainly interested in the role the Inns played for that section of the student body with courtly ambition. Commenting on the Inns' wider educational role as a finishing school, Philip J. Finkelpearl notes that, »[i]t is difficult to ascertain exactly when such a use … arose«, although he suggests that »it was essentially a product of Elizabeth's reign«.[4] Part of a wider Tudor education system which catered for an increasing demand for young men to become bureaucrats and diplomats, and responding to the changing world of sixteenth-century government, the Inns became from the 1530s onwards an educational route for those ambitious to become part of this courtly and poli-

3 Jayne Elisabeth Archer, Elizabeth Goldring and Sarah Knight (eds.), *The Intellectual and Cultural World of the Early Modern Inns of Court*, Manchester: Manchester University Press 2011. See also recent work on this area in *REED: Inns of Court*, eds. Alan H Nelson and John R Elliott, Jr., Cambridge 2010, and Jessica Winston, »Literary Associations of the Middle Temple«, in: Richard O. Havery (ed.), *The History of the Middle Temple*, Oxford and Portland, Oregon 2011.

4 Philip J. Finkelpearl, *John Marston of the Middle Temple*, Cambridge, Mass: Harvard University Press 1969, p. 11.

tical world. One recent commentator demonstrates the »remarkable invasion of the universities by established and would-be gentry« which was suggestive of increased social mobility and this widening of the social groups participating in the life of both the universities and the Inns led to the need in the latter for training beyond the law.[5] If a young man of modest background, but with sufficient intellect, were to thrive at court, he would need to ›appear‹ to belong there and to play his role convincingly.

In the late Elizabethan period all four Inns provided a largely consistent kind of education for their members. The formal training was similar in style to that of the universities, and as legal historian J. H. Baker tells us:

> The division of exercises into lectures and disputed cases reflected the educational system in the universities, and it resulted in a parallel graduation system. Utter barristers, corresponding with bachelors, were those who took part in disputations by arguing cases in hall as if at the bar of a court ...[6]

The means of assessment in both kinds of institution, therefore – university and Inns of Court – was ultimately a judgement of a man's verbal dexterity. The quality of that education has been questioned, and Wilfred Prest, another historian of the Inns, has argued that the very ineffectiveness of formal teaching at the Inns led to an emphasis on extra-curricular activities and made them conducive environments for literary pursuits.[7] However this may be, the focus on rhetoric was clearly paramount and all activities for legal students reflected the need for skill in this area. As Jessica Winston points out, Sidney, in *The Defence of Poesy*, »compares the poet to the lawyer ... because both are skilled in the art of persuasion«[8], and legal education, verbal training and literary aspiration are thereby seen to exist in a symbiotic relationship.

Yet the importance of verbal skill is, throughout, linked with a focus on the visual. One famous Middle Templar, Henry Wotton, gained his degree aged 20 at Queen's College, Oxford, with a viva which presented a range of arguments concerning the workings of the eye. The event was recorded and lauded by his biographer Isaak Walton, who noted that the future diplomat performed so well, it was »so exactly debated, and so rhetorically heightened, as, among other admirers, caused the learned Italian, Albericus Gentilis, then Professor of the Civil

5 Frank Whigham, *Ambition and Privilege: The Social Tropes of Elizabethan Courtesy Theory*, Berkeley 1984, p. 12

6 J. H. Baker, »The third university 1450 – 1550: law school or finishing school?«, in: *The Intellectual and Cultural World of the Early Modern Inns of Court* (as note 3), p. 17.

7 *The Inns of Court under Elizabeth I and the Early Stuarts, 1590 – 1640*, London 1972, p. 168.

8 Jessica Winston, »Literary Associations of the Middle Temple«, in: *The History of the Middle Temple* (as note 3), p. 152.

Law in Oxford, to call him ›Henrice mi Ocelle‹«.[9] Proceeding to London, and the Inns, Wotton would thus have found a similar system of learning in place. A modern scholar might also find interest in his choice of university debate. The importance of sight, both observations of others and the spectacle one presented to the world, was supreme in a culture which judged so regularly by visual as well as verbal evidence. As one recent commentator has explained, »[p]articipation in the life of the Middle Temple, including as a spectator, provided one way to discern patters of juridical interpretation …«[10], and it was clearly important for a young man to observe the performance of others, as well as to develop verbal skills. Wotton's attempt to understand the mechanics of seeing is, with hindsight, highly appropriate for a man who was to observe so acutely in his letters the appearance and actions of those around him, and whose career was to show the danger of being overlooked. Indeed, his life within court circles gives evidence of the importance of both the verbal and the visual. Fluent in many European languages, Wotton's verbal dexterity was a great asset in his work as the Earl of Essex's secretary in the last years of the 1590s. However, it was also to cause him great difficulty in his later relationship with James I, who was not at all impressed by his punning comment in a friend's commonplace book: »An ambassador is an honest man sent to lie [reside] abroad for the good of his country«. Writing it in Latin, the play on the verb (rendered »mentiendum«) disappeared and this led to several months of Wotton kicking his heels in London while he waited for the king's forgiveness. In visual rather than verbal terms, however, he had earlier been notably more successful with James. Assuming the disguise of an Italian merchant, Ottavio Baldi, rather in the manner of a dramatic device, Wotton had travelled to the King's Scottish court as early as 1600, successfully gained entrance and impressed the man who was soon to be the English monarch.[11]

Young men like Wotton, from good families but not of the nobility, found that time at the Inns allowed them to thrive after their studies both in the legal world and in positions which relied on preferment from someone at court. An explicit reference to such rising comes in one example of the manuals available

9 Isaak Walton, *Walton's Lives of Dr. John Donne, Sir Henry Wotton, Mr. Richard Hooker, Mr. George Herbert and Dr. Robert Sanderson*, London 1888, pp. 110-111.

10 Damian X. Powell, »The Inns of Court and the common law mind: the case of James Whitelocke«, in: *The Intellectual and Cultural World of the Early Modern Inns of Court* (as note 3), p. 78.

11 For details of Wotton's life, see A. J. Loomie's article in the *Oxford Dictionary of National Biography* <http://www.oxforddnb.com/view/article/30001?docPos=1> [accessed 28 February 2013], and Sir Isaak Walton's account (as note 9), though both of these unfortunately omit to mention Wotton's entrance to Middle Temple. This is however clear from the entry of »Henry Wotton, of Bowghton Malherbe, Kent., esq.« listed on 12 August, 1595, in the *Register of Admissions to the Honorable Society of the Middle Temple*, London 1949, Vol. I, p. 69.

for young men at the time, John Hoskins' *Directions for Speech and Style*. Probably written while Hoskins was himself studying for the bar, in the late 1590s, the text is dedicated from »the dearest lover of your well-doings« to the unnamed son of a fellow Middle Templar. In his dedication, Hoskins makes clear his aspirations on the young man's behalf, hoping to forward his »many virtuous hopes« by advice on improving his verbal and written performance. Instructing the young man on the relationship between the »conceits of the mind« and the tongue which »is interpreter of those pictures«, he warns his dedicatee that a man's mind will not »be thought in tune whose words do jar«. The analogies by which he advances his argument, though, expose his expectations of the Templar's social advancement:

> Were it an honor to a prince to have the majesty of his embassage spoiled by a careless ambassador? And is it not as great an indignity that an excellent conceit and capacity by the indiligence of an idle tongue should be defaced?[12]

Hoskins' desire, shared with the student's father, »to make somewhat more of you than one of my young masters of the Temple« chimes in well with the increased social mobility of the Tudor age, and the part that the Inns played in the ability of aspirant young men to rise into courtly and governmental roles. William Harrison discusses the rising of the yeoman class in his *Historical Description* and gives evidence of the role played by the Inns, within the wider educational context of Tudor England, noting:

> many [yeomen] are able and do buy the lands of unthrifty gentlemen, and often sending their sons to the schools, to the universities, and the inns of court, or otherwise leaving them sufficient lands whereupon they may live without labour, do make them by these means to become gentlemen.[13]

There were many examples of men from non-aristocratic backgrounds, whose families had only been part of the gentry for a generation or two, or were not at all ›gentle‹, who throve by these means.

One such Templar destined to rise *through* his legal studies, rather than *around* them, was James Whitelocke, whose career at the Inns, and his fascinating account of his life, *Liber Famelicus*, has recently been explored by historian Damian Powell. He describes Whitelocke as »[t]he fourth, twin son of a merchant and a classic ›middling sort‹ who saw his chance for Oxford at the Merchant Taylors' School«.[14] Whitelocke's Victorian editor conjures up a man less prepossessing;

12 John Hoskins, *Directions for Speech and Style*, ed. Hoyt H. Hudson, Princeton Studies in English, Vol. 12, Princeton, N. J. 1935. The dedication is on pp. 2-3.

13 William Harrison, »Historical Description«, in: Raphael Holinshed, *The First and second volumes of Chronicles*, London 1587, p. 163, ll. 32-39.

14 Powell (as note 10), p. 77.

unlike his three brothers, one of whom was bound up with the Essex Rebellion and the Gunpowder Plot and another of whom was adventuring with Drake when the great man died, James Whitelocke had a »plodding, steady youth«, »rising from the middle ranks« to become an eminent lawyer.[15] His career, like that of many of his contemporary Innsmen, relied upon the engagement of a patron, and, as Powell explains, »Whitelocke's engagement with the spaces within and beyond the Middle Temple suggest an ambition to rise, as it were, with the barristers, drawing upon the social and professional cachet of his Inn to push forward in society«.[16] This »social and professional cachet« gave many men their start in London and court life; like Whitelocke, many students' engagement with the social and professional space of the Inns of Court allowed them to rehearse and improve their appearance and performance, until they were ready for the demands of the courtly stage.

The early career of Sir Thomas Overbury, a courtier less ›plodding‹ than his Middle Temple contemporary Whitelocke, though of similarly modest birth, is evidence of the means the Inns gave to aspirant young men to rise even if not called to the bar at all. Born to a ›middling‹ family in Warwickshire, his progress from Queen's College, Oxford, to his father's Inn was the route by which he moved to court, and clearly his appearance, as well as his learning, was influential on his success. Becoming first a server in the King's chamber, and reputedly described by Queen Anna as »a prety yong fellow«[17], Overbury was in fewer than ten years to progress to a position where he was the right hand man of Robert Carr, the King's favourite, and was performing the kind of work which allowed Sir Robert Naunton to inform his correspondent, Sir Ralph Winwood, that the delay in appointing a new Principal Secretary at the death of Cecil may be to allow Overbury time to accede to that prestigious post himself.[18]

Clearly for all these men, part of the training the Inns of Court gave them was in developing effective male friendships. Gerard Legh, member of the Inner Temple and author of the curious work *The Accedens of Armory*, dedicated

15 *Liber Famelicus of Sir James Whitelocke, a Judge of the Court of King's Bench in the Reigns of James I and Charles I*, ed. John Bruce, London: Camden Society 1858, p. vi and p. i; original manuscript, BL, Additional MS 53725.

16 Powell (as note 10), p. 77.

17 See the comments of his father, Nicholas Overbury, to his grandson, dated to 1637, in BL Additional Manuscript, 15476, f. 92^{v}.

18 Sir Robert Naunton to Winwood, »[1612] September [15-]25, n.s., Holeborne«, *HMC Buccleuch (Whitehall)*, I, p. 113: »some standers by are apt to conceive that the King meaneth to keep these places in suspense between himself and my Lords of Rochester … and that meanwhile Sir Tho. Overburie may fit himself with as good a probability to furnish the place in time, by the practice and experience he is now in …«

to his fellow Innsmen, saw the friendships men formed in the institutions as important beyond the confines of the Inns themselves; there was, he tells us, »such unitie of minds and manners, as lightly never after is severed, then which is nothinge more profitable to the common-weale«.[19] Clearly this development of friendship meant a lot to the erudite James Whitelocke, as can be seen in the notes he copied in 1619 from the speech he gave upon leaving the Middle Temple for Serjeant's Inn. He showed his awareness of the practical efficacy of such friendships when he declared his regret that, »though I have found yow all my worthye frends, and assure myself of the continuance of your loves, yet I fear that by my remove I shall misse sum of the effects of it«.[20] In his recent essay on Whitelocke, Damian Powell notes that he called his professional cohort »my *coœtanei*, for we began together in the universitye, came hether together, and have lived together ever sithence, and our loves and affections have growen up together«.[21] Many of the influential group of men at the Middle Temple in the late 1590s were bound by a shared university experience at Oxford, after a smaller group had shared their schooling at Winchester.[22] In the context of Cicero's influential text *De Amicitia*, this homosocial society gave its members, ambitious for a life at court, future allies, as well as the ability to develop such close male friendships with those potential patrons who would be vital to their progress. Although perhaps a more extreme example than many, one thinks of the close bond between Thomas Overbury and Robert Carr, the young Scottish nobleman who was to become, as the King's favourite, first Viscount Rochester and then Earl of Somerset.

In a recent essay on the circulation of manuscript poetry at the Inns in the early Elizabethan period, Jessica Winston proposes a mutually formative link between this environment of male friendship and the poetry written and exchanged by its members. She comments that, »lyric poetry at the Inns served a social as well as psychological function, allowing men to enter into, connect with, and shape the social world of the Inns of Court«, and goes on to argue how this participative society allowed men to thrive in the demanding world of the court. The Inns, she comments, »furnished them with the incentive, authorisation and credentials to begin to make contacts in the professional and political world of the Elizabethan

19 *The Accedens of Armory*, London 1576, fol. 119^{v}.

20 *Liber Famelicus* (as note 15), p. 82.

21 Powell (as note 10), p. 75, where, citing *Liber Famelicus* again, he comments that Whitelocke shows the bond between men at the Inn »deepened as ›collegues, for we have lived together ever sithence in the participation of studies, in doing of exercises, in taking our degrees, and for 28 years, almost compleat, have been *collaterals*, and sat on by the others side‹«.

22 John Davies, John Hoskins, Benjamin Rudyerd and Henry Wotton were all educated at Winchester College and then at Oxford, where they found Richard Martin a contemporary. Thomas Overbury followed Davies and Wotton to Queen's a few years later.

government«[23], and the skills developed in writing, speaking and observing were to prove vital in this transition and in their future courtly performance.

Thus the Inns acted as far more than centres of legal training. For several generations of Elizabethan and Jacobean aspirant courtiers, they gave a base from which to discover London, and a congenial environment to build the kind of friendships which would help to support them as they faced the threats of the world beyond, as well as giving them the skills to build productive relationships with potential patrons. Although the importance of verbal dexterity cannot be overestimated in a society so much influenced by humanist education, Gerard Legh gives further evidence that men learned much more there than the ability to use language. Legal scholar, Paul Raffield, discusses Legh's comparison of »the Inner Temple to a Platonic academy«, and explores how the Inns enabled the men who studied there to rise in society. He points out that »members not only learn to govern and to serve their ›prince and common weale‹, but also [quoting Legh again] ›to use all other exercises of bodye and minde whereunto nature most aptly serveth, to adorn by speaking, countenance, gesture, & use of apparel, the person of a gentleman, wherby amitie is obtained and continued‹«.[24] In an essay focused on the use of visual signs and symbols at the Inns, Raffield's evidence demonstrates the conjunction of friendship, rhetorical skills and, importantly, gesture and visual appearance which would allow these young men to fit into the court environment. As the contemporary prevalence of courtier manuals shows, many of these ›gentlemen‹ may not have been quite so gentle before being trained to appear so.

One example of such literature, aiming to decode courtly behaviour, and implicitly enabling access to it for those who are not born to courtly life, is Giovanni Della Casa's *Galateo*. The text has a clear appeal for Inns of Court men, surely one of its most ready audiences, and its subtitle makes clear its aims and intended readership: »A treatise of the manners and behauiours, it behoueth a man to vse and eschewe, in his familiar conuersation. A worke very necessary & profitable for all gentlemen, or other«. As well as the link this subtitle suggests between behaviour and conversation, appearance and language use, it also advertises its intended appeal not simply to those who are already gentlemen but also, perhaps the most likely readers, those who intend to be gentlemen in the future, but are currently »other«. It is found in 1576 first translated into

23 Jessica Winston, »Lyric Poetry at the early Elizabethan Inns of Court«, in: *The Intellectual and Cultural World of the Early Modern Inns of Court* (as note 3), p. 240.

24 Paul Raffield, »The Inner Temple revels (1561 – 1562) and the Elizabethan rhetoric of signs: legal iconography at the early modern Inns of Court««, in: *The Intellectual and Cultural World of the Early Modern Inns of Court* (as note 3), p. 38, quoting The Accedens of Armory, fols. 118v, 119v.

English by Robert Peterson of Lincoln's Inn, dedicated to Robert Dudley, but with prefatory letters of recommendation from fellow Innsmen. Della Casa's advice about dress is typical of the focus placed upon appearance in the text, and of its paternal, advisory tone. He is clear in not encouraging excess. »Your apparell must be shaped according to the fashion of the time, and your calling«, he stresses in Peterson's translation:

> for the causes I have showed you before. For we must not take vpon vs to alter customes at our will... Euery man may applie those fashions, that be in common vse, the moste to his owne aduantage, that he can.[25]

There follows specific advice on what a man should do if his legs are too long, too small, too great, too crooked, and so on, with specific points on length, colour and decoration of garments. One key issue, interestingly, is to avoid wearing »Ganymedes hosen« or »Cupides doublet«: that is to say the kind of clothing that will draw undue and unwanted attention and risks those around believing an aspirant courtier to have ignored his proper »condition or estate«. As in the case of Malvolio – a character rare in being noted by a member of Shakespeare's contemporary audience, who happened also to be a Middle Templar – ambition can lead to ridicule if you choose your attire unwisely.[26]

The importance of appearance, and particularly clothing, was clear through the restrictions the authorities at the Inns tried to impose upon it. Those who attempted to rise from non-aristocratic backgrounds were often members alongside scions of the nobility, and the difference in the disposable income available to young men of different classes could lead to problems. There was a difficulty, for instance, if the younger sort grew too visible, and, through excesses in their appearance, came to challenge what Powell characterises as »the fragile power relations at work between those lawyers who had risen from middling sorts to great influence in their Inns, and those young grandees who had come to the Inns armed with wealth and influence«.[27] It was not always simply a matter of dressing according to one's estate, clearly, when that might mean that a student appeared to be superior to elder benchers.

The Middle Temple parliament records are interesting in this regard, as they are the official voice of these benchers. There are several records of restriction on

25 Giovanni Della Casa, *Galateo*, trs. Robert Peterson of Lincoln's Inn, London 1576, pp. 108-109.

26 John Manningham's *Diary* gives a famous account of his observations of the 1602 Middle Temple performance of *Twelfth Night*, with a telling focus on the aspirant steward Malvolio. See *Diary of John Manningham of the Middle Temple and of Bradbourne, Kent, Barrister-at-Law, 1602–1603*, ed. John Bruce, Esq., London 1868, p. 18.

27 Powell (as note 10), p. 81.

dress in the latter years of Mary's reign, with precise limits on colour and cut of garments which could be worn by those below the status of Knight, as well as an attempt to restrict imitation of foreign fashions, »on pain of« at first a fine, and then, for a second offence, expulsion. This distinction between aristocratic students and their middling contemporaries demonstrates Powell's point that benchers, themselves mainly not from the aristocracy, had to allow some level of excess in the dress of their better born students. The official restriction on the dress of young men born in less exalted circumstances, though, does perhaps suggest this latter group's illicit attempts to emulate their noble contemporaries. The official records of the later Elizabethan period show much less preoccupation with dress, the only decrees of the 1590s, for instance, asserting a ban on the wearing of boots and cloaks in Hall. At least one Innsman, a Mr. William Younge, was expelled for this, and had to plead for a year before he was restored.[28]

By his choice of examples of how to improve one's verbal skills, John Hoskins exploits the fashionable preoccupations of a young Innsman to secure such a reader's attention; at the same time, he appears to adopt a rather uncharacteristically conformist attitude, as the implications of the text are quite in keeping with official regulation. His illustration of »Division«, in the section of the text headed »To Amplify«, suggests a variant that a successful speaker might substitute for »he apparelleth himself with great discretion«:

> For the stuff, his clothes were more rich than glittering; as for the fashion, rather usual for his sort than fantastical for his invention; for colour, more grave and uniform than wild and light; for fitness, made as well for eases of exercise as to set forth to the eye those parts which in him had most excellency.[29]

Although the treatise is not giving explicit advice about clothing, and may even be ›tongue in cheek‹, the *exemplum* glances at inappropriate gaudiness (»Ganymedes hosen« or »Cupides doublet«?), as well as issues of colour which, in a manner reminiscent of sumptuary law, can suggest or negate moral value, and the power of clothing to demonstrate a man's physical attributes. It thus demonstrates some of the specific preoccupations with appearance and dress which were key for the aspirant Innsman.

The potential for sartorial excess is demonstrated in the will of one of the Middle Temple's early Jacobean playwrights, the promising figure of Edward Shar-

28 *Middle Temple Records*, ed. Charles Henry Hopwood, London 1904, Vol. I. For references to Marian restrictions, see p. 110 (entry for 12 May 1557), p. 111 (25 June 1557) and p. 116 (20 May 1558). For an example of the more limited Elizabethan records, see p. 358 (entry for 21 November 1595).

29 *Directions* (as note 12), p. 23.

pham, who was to die of plague in 1608, aged approximately 32 and apparently in debt to his tailor. Having produced two extant plays, one for the Blackfriars boys company in 1605/6, and the second for the Children of the King's Revels at the Whitefriars in early 1607, Sharpham was a satirical voice on court and Inns life. His will, however, reminds us of the potential for the middling sorts themselves to wear clothing which exceeded the recommendations of an advisor such as Della Casa, and reveals a flamboyance which came in part from a connection with the playhouse. To his brother, Sharpham left »my damson Colloured Cloake lined throughe w*i*th blacke veluett and my Rapyer beinge hatched with syluer, and a girdle and hangers trymed with syluer belonginge to the same« and to his male cousin, »my palle Carnac*i*on sylke stocking*es*«.[30] As another satirical writer put it, clothing demonstrated the change from university student to law student: the Inns of Court man »is distinguished from a Scholler by a paire of silke stockings and a Beauer Hat«.[31]

All of this makes clear the importance of appearances and the need for aspirational young men to make a suitable show if they planned a court career, and James's accession to the English throne seems only to have increased this. A letter from Thomas Howard to Sir John Harington demonstrates his amused awareness of the young men who are in 1607 moulding their appearance to please their monarch. Howard advises Harington that, if he is to make a successful entry to the court:

> I woud wish you to be well trimmed; get a new jerkin well borderd, and not too short; the King saith, he liketh a flowing garment; be sure it be not all of one sort, but diversly colourd, the collar falling somewhat down, and your ruff well stiffend and bushy. We have lately had many gallants who failed in their suits, for want of due observance of these matters.[32]

Even bearing in mind the nice irony of Howard's letter, which undoubtedly exaggerates the importance of sartorial elegance for comic effect, personal appearance was clearly a pressing concern for aspirant courtiers, and, for those suitably handsome, dressing, as Hoskins had put it, »to set forth to the eye those parts which in him had most excellency« had now become a vital means to courtly advancement. Howard is more than aware of James I's enjoyment of a such a young man, and notes that approximately three years after his accession:

30 E. A. J. Honigman and Susan Brock, *Playhouse Wills, 1558 – 1642: An edition of wills by Shakespeare and his contemporaries in the London theatre*, Manchester 1993, p. 78.

31 *New and Choise Characters of seuerall Authors Together with that exquisite and vnmatcht Poeme, The Wife, written by Syr Thomas Ouerburie*, London 1615, sig. I6^r.

32 *The Letters and Epigrams of Sir John Harington*, ed. Norma Egbert McClure, Philadelphia 1930, p. 32.

> The King is nicely heedfull of such points, and dwelleth on good looks and handsome accoutrements.Eighteen servants were lately discharged,and many more will be discarded, who are not to his liking in these matters.

In describing the progress of the rising favourite, Robert Carr, Howard notes that he »doth much study all art and device« in his pursuit of preferment, suggestive of the self-consciousness and planning in Carr's success. This »art and device« has apparently involved »chang[ing] his tailors and tiremen many times« and joining in the king's mockery of »long grown fashion[s]« amongst young English courtiers. For an Innsman considering employment at the royal court, clearly how he dressed was going to be important, and, even if it irritated the older benchers who considered fashionable excesses counter to the regulations of the Inns, he was going to have to develop a style and appearance which would make sure he was noticed.

Although the matter of courtly dress was clearly vital, being a member of the Inns allowed an ambitious young man access to sources of advice and example as to how he might be costumed for his role. In other issues of appearance, though, such as appropriate behaviour and gesture, what one might term the ›acting skills‹ necessary for success, the Inns' organized extra-curricular activities gave more direct guidance. The masques and revels which were a compulsory part of a student's learning activities provided those who did want to progress to such a career with many of the skills to do so.

Revels had long formed part of entertainment at the Inns. Early accounts of the Christmas revels can be found in the late fifteenth century, mentioning »[b] esides the musical and alimentary entertainments« several »zoological displays«, and references to »disguisings«. Importantly, even by 1450 there is mention of »A mock royal court, with a student king«.[33] The desire for a Christmas season with a Master of the Revels or a Lord of Misrule is clear from several entries in the 1590s Middle Temple parliament records, where students, after some years when such festivities had been banned due to plague, decided to take matters into their own hands. One such incident in 1591 demonstrates the role of appearance, here »disguisings«, in their boisterous behaviour:

> In spite of the orders against a Lord of Misrule on Candlemas night, divers gentlemen of the House on last Candlemas night … were expelled ... for breaking the said orders, and broke open chamber doors and abused many gentlemen of the House, as appears by the examination of townsmen who were with them, and some of this Fellowship knew them notwithstanding their disguised attire ...[34]

33 Baker (as note 6), p. 13.

34 *Middle Temple Records* (as note 28), p. 318.

Breaking into rooms and demanding payment for the Master of the Revels led to some serious punishments, though one can see that the disguises were effective as, some months afterwards, there is another record that, although his partner in crime, John Davies is to be readmitted to the Inn:

> Mr. Jacobb must reveal those whom he knew to be of the disordered company on Candlemas night last, before he receive any favour.[35]

Yet the revels were clearly perceived to be part of the learning environment, as well as being entertaining. A report on the Inns written around 1540 by Sir Nicholas Bacon, Thomas Denton and Robert Cary to inform Henry VIII of the their workings, describes how, if it is not a time of sickness, the Inns hold a »solemn Christmas«, for which:

> they appoint and chose certain of the house to be Officers, and bear certain rules in the house during the said time, which Officers for the most part are such, as are exercised in the King's Highness house, and other Noble men.

The writers of the report defend participation in the revels on the grounds that the students imitate offices of state in them »onely to the intent, that they should in time to come know how to use themselves«.[36] Philip J. Finkelpearl, setting the context for his exploration of the Gray's Inn's revels of 1594/5, the *Gesta Grayorum*, decides that, »[w]e will probably come close to the true tone of the revels if we see them as a mixture of disorderly conduct, mock solemnity, and a serious miming of dignified roles«.[37]

All of this implies that the time spent at the Inns was a transitional one, where young men learnt the art of courtiership through a kind of dramatic mimicry. The worlds of Inns and royal court overlapped, and one place where this was clearly seen was in the Inns' masques and revels, elements of which formed courtly entertainment, too. In the audience of the *Gesta Grayorum* were the earl of Essex, Robert Cecil and the earl of Southampton, and in a dedicatory letter of 1598 to Essex's sister, Penelope Rich, Bartholomew Yong discusses her presence at the Middle Temple revels, along with »many noble Lordes and faire Ladies«, who »graced and beautified those sportes«.[38]

The interplay between court, Inns and revels dramatic performance is worth considering more closely at this point. The *Gesta Grayorum*, for example, had

35 Ibid., p. 328 (5 May 1592).

36 Edward Waterhouse, *Fortescutus Illustratus*, London 1663, p. 546.

37 Finkelpearl (as note 4), p. 38.

38 *REED: Inns of Court*, eds. Alan H Nelson and John R Elliott, Jr., Cambridge 2010, Vol. I, p. 130.

as its sovereign the Prince of Purpoole, the name a pun on the ancient manor of Portpoole where the Inn had its site. The Prince, we are told:

> reigned for a full six weeks, served by some forty officers and dozens more followers. In this time, [he] made a royal progress through the city; issued formal pardons for licentious behaviour within his realm; received official letters from subordinate rulers [and so on].[39]

Clearly dramatic performance, and by the 1590s the performance of professional drama, was a vital part of all revels, and there are scholarly arguments put forward that both *A Comedy of Errors* and *Twelfth Night* may have been written for this Inn's audience, not merely acted before them.[40] Yet the performative aspect of the revels appears not to have been limited to the selected play, to professional players, or even to a scripted narrative.

A closer look at the records of the Middle Temple *Prince D'Amour* revels of 1597 – 1598 shows the roles played by Templars during this festive season. The Prince, Richard Martin (one of those expelled for his ›misrule‹ in 1591) reigned over a Christmas court of his fellow law students, a talented group with a satirical bent. Benjamin Rudyerd's account of the revels period, published in 1660, records not merely the performance ›script‹, but, in a highly comical manner, how the Christmas court took shape and what events revealed about the characters at Middle Temple at that point in time. Key amongst this group is John Davies, or, as he is often labelled in the text, Stradilax. His behaviour illustrates well for our purposes an exaggerated version of the performative skills life at the Inns promoted. His appearance on Christmas Eve, for instance, »in a Marmelad-Colour-Taffata Gown« suggests a man with the desire to attract attention.[41] Perhaps, since we are told it »was never seen after«, the response to his flamboyance led him to believe it verged on »Cupides doublet«; even at the Christmas court of the Prince D'Amour, one could apparently misjudge one's clothing.

39 Bradin Cormack, »Locating *The Comedy of Errors*: revels jurisdiction at the Inns of Court«, in: *The Intellectual and Cultural World of the Early Modern Inns of Court* (as note 3), p. 275.

40 In the case of *Twelfth Night*, John Dover Wilson proposed a first performance of the play at the 1602 Middle Temple revels in his edition with Arthur Quiller-Couch, Cambridge 1930, p. 95; it has been more recently argued by Anthony Arlidge, *Shakespeare and the Prince of Love: The Feast of Misrule at the Middle Temple*, London 2000. The likelihood is discussed, and the idea largely dismissed, by Keir Elam in his Arden 3 edition, London: Arden Shakespeare 2008, p. 95. The suggestion that *The Comedy of Errors* was written for the Gray's Inn performance in 1594 was made in 1956 in Sidney Thomas's essay, »The Date of *The Comedy of Errors*«, in: *Shakespeare Quarterly*, VII, pp. 377-384. The case is discussed in the Arden 2 edition of the play, ed. R. A. Noakes, London: Arden Shakespeare 1963, p. xxi, and it has been more recently developed in Bradin Cormack's essay cited above (as note 39).

41 Benjamin Rudyerd, *Le Prince D'Amour or The Prince of Love*, London 1660, p. 82.

Appearance and rhetoric are equally part of Davies's performance. In order to gain the support of his peers in his bid to be Prince of the revels, he decides to strike a memorable posture. It is said that he:

> ran down amongst them, like *Laocoon ardens*, and with a most furious and turbulent action, uttered these two Proverbs, the one borrowed from a Smith, the other from a Clown. *My Masters strike while the Iron is hot: Make hay while the Sun shineth.*[42]

Having been immediately rejected in favour of his then friend, Martin, and after this first performance which was presumably inside the Hall, he then takes his highly visible stage outside. Readers are told that »[t]hen *Stradilax* stept up upon the stone Staires in the Porch of the Temple-Hall, from whence nothing but Oysters ever opened their mouthes with eloquence, and spake as follows …«. But he is unable to complete what begins as an ornate piece of oratory, for »they went to bed, and so he did not tell them«. Rudyerd's recording of the two incidents could be argued to show some success on Davies's part. Despite the ridicule implied by the exaggerated lexis and the mock-heroic comparison to Laocoon, he is observed by all, and is an object of all spectators. However, his ability to gain the notice of the entire Inn is marred by the failure of his utterances. The two proverbs, »one borrowed from a Smith, the other from a Clown«, allow Rudyerd to joke at the expense of his lowly origins and he becomes a figure of fun, subsequently comparable to an Oyster in his lack of eloquence, and just as ineffective.

As the drama of the »mock royal court« began in earnest, Martin's courtiers, personated by, amongst others, John Hoskins, John Davies, Charles Best and Benjamin Rudyerd, adopted their parodied roles of state. One by one the Secretary, President, Lord Chancellor, Lord Marshall and so on are given their duties in this short-lived kingdom. The duties are clearly humorous variants of the real responsibilities of such figures; the Treasurer, for example, is:

> to receive all the Revenews of the Crown; as Sighs, Sonnets, Tears, Vows, Protestations &c. and to give allowance and Pensions out of them to all such as desire them …[43]

The revels variant often appears to act in parodic echo of the original; for instance, when presented with a challenger knight who wishes to enter into trial by combat, the Prince is defended by the protective intervention of a rhetorically able, if verbose, Secretary, who argues at great length against entry into war, as both Cecils, father and son, had done at the court of Elizabeth. There appears

42 Ibid., p. 79.
43 Ibid., p. 25.

to be a whiff of political satire here, in the latter years of the sixteenth century when the earl of Essex and his followers continued to argue for a more hawkish military policy and engagement with Spanish forces. In other roles, the humour is more general, reliant on the double entendre one might expect of a young men's ›revue‹. The Lord Admiral, for example, is reminded in his list of responsibilities, that »he shall take heed for bearing too much sail, least he spring his Mast, or perish his Main Yard«.[44] It is likely that the earl of Essex, whose house bordered the Middle Temple on the western edge, was in the audience for the revels. He is listed as being present at the *Gesta Grayorum* three years earlier, his sister, Penelope Rich, was addressed shortly afterwards as one present at the Middle Temple revels and he was certainly in England at this point, having just been rewarded by the Queen with the revival of the ancient title Earl Marshal. In the revels, the Prince D'Amour's Earl Marshal is advised to be careful, as his »Truncheon will be the worse for ordering of single Combats, and the greatness of his place will distract his Carriage many ways«. Without straying into open insult, the revels clearly sail close to the wind with satirical comments which can be applied to some very important individuals.

Thus, I would suggest, as well as showing the desire to train students in the arts of the court, demonstrating conformity with the political system they parody, the revels also strike a more transgressive note. Paul Raffield sees the Inns' »invisible curriculum« – from poetry and plays to masques and dining rituals – as reinforcing a specific institutional identity. Focusing on the significance of Middle Temple Hall, he argues that it:

> was the setting for the continuous and undeviating repetition of legal ritual. Participation in these ceremonial rites affirmed the faith of students and practitioners in the legitimacy of the common law. Such rites were exclusive: only members of the Inn could practise them on a regular basis.[45]

And that institutional identity was strongly individual. One might think of Pierre Bourdieu's theory that the educative process is actually one of marking out different social groups; a process which Bourdieu calls »acts of consecration« or »acts of institution«. Bourdieu explains that such a rite »separate[s] those who have undergone it, not from those who have not yet undergone it, but from those who will not undergo it in any sense, and thereby institute[s] a lasting difference between those to whom the rite pertains and those to whom it does not pertain«.[46] In other words, the education at the Inns marked out Innsmen as an exclusive group with shared knowledge and experiences: a group rehearsing

44 Ibid., p. 27.
45 Paul Raffield, *Images and Cultures of Law*, Cambridge 2004, p. 43.
46 Pierre Bourdieu, (see note 2), p. 117.

the performance of power in preparation for joining the wider courtly or governmental elite. Yet it would be a mistake to see this rehearsal as merely conforming to the expectations of others; as products of this process of preparation, Innsmen clearly saw themselves as members of strongly independent institutions.

Recent work by Lynne Magnusson on a play clearly influenced by Shakespeare's knowledge of the Inns of Court, *Love's Labour's Lost*, explores further consequences of this institutional identity. Using a version of a paradigm for identifying a speech community, originally developed by linguist Dell Hymes, to examine the shared characteristics of members of the Inns of Court, she analyzes the impact of such a background on the language of Innsmen, and proposes what she terms »scoff power« as a key linguistic feature both at the Inns and in Shakespeare's play.[47] As with all in-group language, one of the effects is to exclude those not of the group, and thus, as Bourdieu suggested, mark out further the difference between those who have undergone training at the Inns from those who never will. However, Magnusson argues that »scoff power« is more than a way of excluding others, and in addition, »[w]ith the young lords in *Love's Labour's Lost* as at the Inns of Court, there is strong evidence that mockery and verbal shaming also played an important role in shaping identity in their in-group communication«. Overlapping with the nature and effect of the revels, the use of satire and flyting helps to define what the group actually is; that is, as well as overtly prestigious language and verbal conformity allowing social progress, as argued above, an Innsman's language also defines the group against the rest of the world, those both superior and inferior socially.

It is interesting too that Magnusson draws attention to the quasi-dramatic nature of language in many of the situations which train and define a student's verbal usage, and thus implies a visual, as well as a verbal, context. As well as participation in the revels, she considers principal discourse events which help a student to refine, and define, his language; these include the expected legal exercises, such as moots and readings, and performance in plays, but also spoken literary events, such verbal satires and put-downs, and discussion at table. Even in this last case, she draws attention to the performative element emphasized in contemporary texts, such as Hoskins' *Directions*, where a premium is placed on being »able to govern a table with Discourse«.[48] One final point of interest here is the inclusion amongst the channels by which a man shows his allegiance of the »semiotics of clothing«. The clues, verbal and visual, work together to build

47 Lynne Magnusson, »Scoff Power in *Love's Labour's Lost*«, in: *Shakespeare Survey*, 57 (2004), p. 205. She cites the original work by Dell Hymes, »Models of the Interaction of Language and Social Life«, in: John J. Gumperz and Dell Hymes (eds.) *Directions in Sociolinguistics: The Ethnography of Communication*, 2nd edn., Oxford 1986, pp. 35-37.

48 Ibid. p. 206.

the effective Innsman, and enable the development of courtiership. The events to which Magnusson refers mainly take place in the public spaces of the Inn, and, as Raffield argues[49], whether a student is a participant or spectator, the location is important in reinforcing the institutional nature of such a performance. Entry into Middle Temple Hall, or the Halls of any of the Inns, must have of itself prompted the adoption of the dress, manner and language expected of a successful performer.

Despite the reliance on courtly patronage which many of Innsmen were to experience in their future lives, their institutional identity encouraged their perception of themselves as subtly distinct from other forms of power. The Inns were liberties, on the edge of the City of London but not under the jurisdiction of the Lord Mayor; in fact they were self-governed. Bradin Cormack has argued that this apparently paradoxical conformity and transgression arises because the revels in fact worked analogously to drama itself, which often, of course, also inhabited liminal spaces on the edge of the city or, as in the players' use of former monastic buildings of Blackfriars or Whitefriars, in self-governing liberties. As the playhouse presented to an audience largely from the city an image of the city and people who inhabited it, so:

> the revels worked as institutional activations of the physical and conceptual space in which the junior members of an Inn now found themselves. The students' fictive reconfiguration of their professional milieu *represents* a political content, but also *enacts* the jurisdictional scene in which delimited action or practice issues in authority.[50]

Hence the revels' pedagogic purpose both emphasizes the desire of Innsmen to perform effectively the role they will need to adopt to succeed at court, and suggests why some Innsmen, I would argue especially some late Elizabethan Middle Templars, found it difficult to fit easily into the demands of the court.[51]

Thus the revels can be seen to play a role full of complex positioning and influence. In a conclusion which builds on Bradin Cormack's perception of the Inns as both conforming and transgressive, Charles Whitney argues that Inns of Court men's influence on contemporary drama was such that their participation

49 See note 45.

50 Cormack (as note 39), p. 273. He cites Jean Howard's formulation, that plays helped to »*construct* the city and make it intelligible for those *un*familiar with its places or the uses to which they can be put«; *Theater of a City: The Places of London Comedy, 1598 – 1642*, Philadelphia, PA 2007, p. 23.

51 We might consider Thomas Overbury's imprisonment after refusing the king's proffered ambassadorship or John Hoskins' imprisonment after a speech opposing royal policy in the 1614 parliament.

in the revels was influential on the representative nature of early modern theatre as a whole. As writers, audience members and readers of plays Innsmen were clearly an important feature in the theatrical landscape; however if one tries to assess not merely their prevalence, which varies from playhouse to playhouse, but their influence, it can be argued that they had a formative impact on the development of much early modern drama. A consequence of this argument may well be to see the revels, a key part of the dramatic preparation of such men, as both reflective of, and influential upon, the contemporary stage. Indeed, as Whitney explores the connection between the revels and the nature of their response to theatre, he concludes, »[t]he customary theatrical festivities of the Inns of Court contributed to the commercial theatre's emphasis on the agency of representation, on the players and other aspects of production as part of the same world as the audience«.[52] Since Paul Raffield notes in addition that »members of the Inns during this period often performed their entertainments before the exclusive audience of the royal court«, this reveals a complex condition of influence, response and reflection.[53] In terms of the revels, it suggests that, at one and the same time, they presented the Inn to its members, the courtly position to aspirant students, and the court to already established courtiers; and that, in some fundamental ways, they both reflected and influenced the drama being presented on the wider public stage.

The blending of Inns of Court and court audiences in this way develops our earlier understanding of what Damian Powell called »the cultural and literary pursuits which tied the Inns … to the artistic orbit of the royal court«.[54] The dividing line between the two becomes blurred, as it must do in a society where leading members of the Queen's government have been at one time members of an Inn, and leading Benchers work alongside court and parliament in the business of the country. Aspirant young Innsmen, desirous of being part of that courtly apparatus and benefitting from Tudor social mobility, did not have far to look to see men who had done just that. But those of the Inns who observed this process in action, writing as they did in the acerbic satirical environment which produced the biting wit of the *Poetomachia*, often wrote scathingly of what they saw.

In conclusion, and as illustration, I now return to my title quotation from John Marston's *Scourge of Villainy*. His tenth and final satire in this vituperative attack on many sections of early modern society addresses members of »faire Albions youth« in turn, and outlines their respective sensualities and foibles.

52 Charles Whitney, *Early Responses to Renaissance Drama*, Cambridge 2006, p. 125.

53 Raffield (as note 24), p. 39.

54 Powell (as note 10), p. 81.

Beginning with Curio, representative of fellow Middle Templar John Davies[55], Marston goes on to examine a lover of fencing, another who cannot forebear to tell jokes and record them in his table-book, and yet another, a lover of the newest fashions, who appears to exemplify those men advised by Della Casa and his ilk. One of this catalogue is a young man Marston names Luscus, whose passion for playgoing, like the others' passions, takes over his entire existence:

> *Luscus* what's playd to day? fayth now I know
> I see thy lips abroach, from whence doth flow
> Naught but pure *Iuliet* and *Romeo*.
> Say, who acts best? *Drusus*, or *Roscio*?
> Now I haue him, that nere of ought did speake
> But when of playes or Plaiers he did treate.
> H'ath made a common-place booke out of playes,
> And speakes in print, at least what ere he sayes
> Is warranted by Curtaine *plaudites* …
> He writes, he rails, he iests, he courts, what not,
> And all from his huge long-scraped stock
> Of well penn'd plays.[56]

In his comments on Luscus, as in those on the other young men he lists, Marston observes the young men of his acquaintance who are the subject of this paper; Innsmen whose lives are preparing them for careers mainly outside the legal world, and whose wider accomplishments, the Inns' »invisible curriculum«, will help them gain preferment. Marston's portrayal is, of course, a satirical one, mocking the passions of his victims, which leads them to time »wholy spent / In that which is but Gentries ornament«. Yet this is just the point. Luscus's obsession with playgoing, and his use of his »huge long-scrap'd stock« of examples to help him »write … rail … iest … court … what not«, is an illustration of the manner by which young Innsmen prepared to perform as courtiers. Through their experience of the often parodic and satirical drama at the finishing school that was the Inns of Court, men such as Thomas Overbury, Henry Wotton, John Donne, and John Davies learnt the visual and verbal skills they needed for the serious business of acting on the courtly stage. They also, as Marston demonst-

55 Though Marston assures his reader in his address »To the Peruser« that »I am free from endeavouring to blast any private mans good name but if any one … will turne it home and say Tis I, I cannot hinder him. Neither doe I injure him«, there can be little doubt from the reference to Davies's poem, *Orchestra*, that the lawyer is meant here; in fact the letter which ends the satire is clearly in itself a witty ›defence‹ those who might resent the flyting of the volume. See *The Sourge of Villainy*, London 1599, sig. I3v.

56 Ibid., H4r.

rates, developed the self-awareness to satirize and criticize both the courtly stage and the process which led them there.

Simon Smith

»*Flourish. Enter the King sicke*«

Exploring Kingship through Musical Spectacle in *Richard III*

The music of *Richard III* rarely receives the level of attention given to *Twelfth Night*'s songs, or to the »noyses, Sounds, and sweet aires« of *The Tempest* (3.2.138-9), yet the Folio text of this complex early play preserves no fewer than fourteen explicit musical cues, calling exclusively for trumpets and drums.[1] It would certainly be a mistake to equate the narrow aural palette of *Richard III* with a lack of dramatic sophistication in its music use; in fact, music appears just as deliberately and precisely in the play as it does in John Marston's *Sophonisba*, or in *The Tempest*, despite these later works making a far greater demand on playhouse musical resources. Perhaps most significantly, amongst various drum and trumpet cues, the final four acts of *Richard III* each contain one royal entrance announced formally with a trumpet call, introducing the four monarchs represented in the play: Edward IV (2.1), Edward V (3.1), Richard III (4.2) and Henry VII (5.8). In early performances, these four trumpet calls would momentarily remake the playhouse as an imagined courtly space, into which the royal figure enters. Notably, the playhouse was unusual in offering such spectacles of kingship to audiences without requiring the presence of an actual ruler. This conjunction of sound and sight was central, I argue, to the play's impact in early performance, for by punctuating the play with musically announced royal entrances, Shakespeare asked his playhouse audiences to consider repeatedly what kingship could – or

I am extremely grateful to Hannah August, Jackie Watson and Sue Wiseman for reading and commenting on early drafts of this article.

1 Bruce R. Smith's consideration of the various volume and pitch levels in the speech and other sounds of *Richard III* is a notable exception to this trend. See: *The Acoustic World of Early Modern England: Attending to the O-Factor*, Chicago, IL 1999, pp. 229-232. Particularly valuable recent considerations of music in *Twelfth Night* and *The Tempest* include: David Lindley, *Shakespeare and Music*, London 2006, pp. 199-233; Bruce R. Smith, »Ragging *Twelfth Night*: 1602, 1996, 2002-3«, in: Barbara Hodgdon and W. B. Worthen (eds.), *A Companion to Shakespeare and Performance*, Chichester 2005, pp. 57-78; Joseph M. Ortiz, *Broken Harmony: Shakespeare and the Politics of Music*, Ithaca, NY 2011, pp. 164-179. All Shakespearean quotations are from the 1623 Folio unless otherwise indicated. I preserve original spelling and punctuation, silently modernizing usage of i, j, u and v. Act, scene and line numbers are cited in the text here and throughout, and keyed to: Gary Taylor and Stanley Wells (eds.), *William Shakespeare: The Complete Works*, 2. ed., Oxford 2005.

should – look like. However, these dramaturgical intentions only become clear in light of the early modern cultural context that shaped playhouse encounters with the play. In order to reconstruct these intentions, we must first ask how an early audience would have understood and engaged with the playhouse sounds of the trumpet.

Those who inhabited the soundscape of 1590s London would have closely associated the distinctive sounds of trumpets and drums with the outdoor playhouses of Bankside and Shoreditch.[2] Indeed, in November 1596, when theatrical entrepreneur James Burbage planned to bring the performance practices of Shakespeare and his colleagues indoors, the potential migration of these musical sounds from the margins of the city to the Blackfriars precinct drew immediate objections. Whilst Burbage's new playhouse at Blackfriars was still under construction, thirty-one prospective neighbours – somewhat embarrassingly including the company's own patron, George Carey – complained to the Privy Council. Notably, alongside both fears of »vagrant and lewde persons« who would »worke all manner of mischeefe«, and concerns about the spread of disease, the Blackfriars residents objected to just one anticipated performance feature of the plays themselves:

> the same playhouse is so neere the Church that the noyse of the drummes and trumpetts will greatly disturbe and hinder both the ministers and parishioners in tyme of devine service and sermons[.][3]

The petitioners were undoubtedly apprehensive about the loudness of these instruments, and indeed play-text evidence suggests that when the King's Men eventually began performing at Blackfriars after 1609, they did so with the softer cornett replacing the trumpet.[4] However, I suggest that the anticipated disruption to »both the ministers and parishioners« had rather more cultural specificity than a simple issue of volume might indicate. To early modern ears, drum and trumpet calls had extremely precise significations that were often integral to the narrative of dramatic performance. In scenes of war, the sounds of an alarm or a charge communicated the progress of a battle to playhouse attendees; elsewhere, trumpet flourishes or sennets informed the audience that a character of royal status was about to make a formal entrance. To listeners familiar with these conventions,

2 See: Smith, *Acoustic World* (as note 1), pp. 217-222.

3 »November 1596, Petition to the Privy Council by 31 Blackfriars residents«, quoted in: Andrew Gurr, *The Shakespeare Company, 1594 – 1642*, Cambridge 2004, p. 248.

4 For instance, *The Two Noble Kinsmen*, »presented at the Blackfriers by the Kings Majesties servants«, contains ten cues for »cornets«, including a »florish of cornets«, but calls only once for »Trompets«. John Fletcher and William Shakespeare, *The Two Noble Kinsmen*, London 1634, pp. 1-83.

such calls are not just sounds, but bearers of extremely specific meaning. It therefore seems likely that, if played sufficiently loudly in the Blackfriars playhouse, such calls would indeed »greatly disturbe and hinder« local churchgoers who were familiar with playhouse conventions, drawing their thoughts away from God and towards the dramatic narrative unfolding nearby. This response is perhaps analogous to the more recent phenomenon of a familiar television theme tune reverberating through a poorly insulated wall. Of course, the musical sounds of *Richard III* did not actually reach Blackfriars until well into the seventeenth century, remaining at outdoor playhouses including the Theatre and the Globe until 1609, but the issue of the trumpet's cultural resonances that perhaps motivated the Blackfriars complainants is key to understanding Shakespeare's dramaturgical intentions in the play.[5] Significantly, if previous experiences of a particular sound frame later encounters with that same sound, then we can reconsider the music of *Richard III* in light of the associations and expectations that the »noyse of the drummes and trumpetts« would have evoked for early modern subjects. I argue that throughout the play, Shakespeare repeatedly uses trumpet calls announcing royal entrance to raise certain expectations, before directly challenging these expectations in the spectacle of kingship that meets the audience's gaze.

The use of trumpets to announce the entrance of a character with royal or extremely high status was a fully codified convention of the early modern playhouse.[6] Unfortunately however, printed play-texts are often vague about the particular call required, simply specifying »trumpets«. Helpfully, some texts are more specific, containing explicit directions for a »flourish«, »sennet«, or »tucket«.[7] Whilst no reliable English source survives for the music of these military-derived calls, Christopher R. Wilson and Michela Calore note circumstantial evidence suggesting that »the flourish is the most improvisatory and musically least structured« of these signals, whilst continental texts suggest that the sennet

5 The play remained in the repertory of the Lord Chamberlain's/ King's Men throughout their existence between 1594 and 1642, with Richard Burbage renowned for his portrayal of the title role. However, its precise date of composition in the early 1590s, and the identity of the playing company or companies who performed it before the Lord Chamberlain's Men, remains the subject of much critical debate. James R. Siemon offers a cogent summary of the evidence available, and the various histories proposed by scholars, in his recent edition of the play. James R. Siemon (ed.), *Richard III*, The Arden Shakespeare Third Series, London 2009, pp. 45-51.

6 See: Christopher R. Wilson and Michela Calore, *Music in Shakespeare: A Dictionary*, London 2005, pp. 178-182, 376-379, 443-446; Christopher R. Wilson, *Shakespeare's Musical Imagery*, London 2011, p. 71; Frances Ann Shirley, *Shakespeare's Use of Off-Stage Sounds*, Lincoln, NE 1963, p. 71.

7 See: Wilson and Calore (as note 6); Alan C. Dessen and Leslie Thomson, *A Dictionary of Stage Directions in English Drama, 1580 – 1642*, Cambridge 1999, pp. 94, 191, 239.

was notated precisely, and more complex.[8] However, even if the notes of the English calls are absent, fascinating insight into the signification of these signals is preserved in Gervase Markham's *The Souldiers Accidence* (1625). In his manual of infantry and cavalry practice, he explains that in the context of a military drill, a tucket »being heard simplie of it selfe without addition, Commands nothing but a Marching after the Leader«.[9] This signal seems to have been used theatrically to mark the entrance of characters who are of significance, but not of the very highest status, such as the Duke of Cornwall and Goneril in *King Lear*.[10] Elsewhere, in a particularly telling passage, Markham lists »A *Senet* for State« amongst assorted »Other Soundings«, and explains why he is not commenting further on this group of signals: »they have reference to the greater Officers, and those have no need of my Instructions« (I3ᵛ). Markham spends much of the book sidestepping the anticipated criticism that he is trying to tell senior military officers how to do their jobs; indeed, he begins a dedication to »his Majesties most Honorable Councell of Warre« by exclaiming, »God forbid there should be in me such an impudent daring« as to suggest that these great men could learn anything at all from the book (A2ʳ). This evasion in fact makes his reference to the sennet even more valuable, for his unwillingness to engage with the signal indicates the level of status that he associates with it just as clearly as does his explanation that the call is »for State«, i. e. announcing royalty. Unsurprisingly then, the sennet generally appears as a dramatic cue when kings such as Henry VI, Lear and Richard III enter.[11] It is not indisputable that this call was in use on the 1590s stage however, for as Wilson and Calore note, the 1608 quarto edition of *King Lear* is the sole Shakespearean text predating the 1623 Folio that cues a sennet, raising questions about the date – and provenance – of the manuscripts upon which these printed texts are based.[12] Interestingly, Markham does not

8 Wilson and Calore (as note 6). A key source is: Magnus Thomsen, »Music Book for Trumpet« (1598), in *The Royal Library E-Manuscripts: Medieval and Renaissance* <http://www.kb.dk/en/nb/materialer/haandskrifter/HA/e-mss/mdr.html> [accessed 5 February 2013]. William Byrd's keyboard suite entitled »The Battaile« may have more to tell us about English military calls than has hitherto been acknowledged. As Christopher Marsh has noted recently of this suite, »[s]uch sources are neither comprehensive nor necessarily reliable, but they are among the most informative that we have«. See: William Byrd, »The Battaile«, in: C. J. F. Cofone (ed.), *Elizabeth Rogers Hir Virginall Booke*, New York 1975, pp. 23-39; Christopher Marsh, »›The Pride of Noise‹: Drums and their Repercussions in Early Modern England«, in: *Early Music* 39 (2011), pp. 203-216 (p. 204).

9 Gervase Markham, *The Souldiers Accidence*, London 1625, sig. I3ʳ. Hereafter cited in the text.

10 Wilson and Calore (as note 6), pp. 443-446.

11 Ibid., pp. 376-379.

12 Ibid., p. 377. The link they suggest between the emergence of the term ›sennet‹ and »the employment [in the seventeenth century] of professional musicians in the theatre (for instance the consort at the Blackfriars)« remains speculative.

mention flourishes at all; the signal is not amongst his six »Poyntes of Warre« that tell »the Horse-troope« when to saddle, mount, stand ready, march, charge, or change watch ($I3^{r-v}$). Nonetheless, it is clear from many extant play-texts that the convention of a flourish announcing the entry of kings and high-ranking noblemen was widespread.[13] Flourishes and sennets are therefore the calls relevant to moments of spectacular royal entrance in early modern playhouses.

Undoubtedly, the widespread theatrical use of such signals would have fostered certain expectations. Upon hearing the sound of a sennet or a flourish, playhouse attendees would become accustomed to the present sight of a figure with the bearing, trappings and other corporeal manifestations of royalty, as far as the actors' skills and the playing company's properties could supply these visual signifiers. Indeed, in the view of Stephen Gosson, this playhouse convention created a deeply threatening separation between the performance of royalty, and the corporeal body of the reigning monarch:

> for a meane person to take upon him the title of a Prince with counterfeit porte, and traine; is by outwarde signes to shewe them selves otherwise then they are, and so with in the compasse of a lye, which by Aristotles judgement is naught of it selfe, and to be fledde.[14]

In fact, it is precisely because stage-kings are not in fact kings that playwrights such as Shakespeare could experiment with the conventions of royal self-presentation. Whilst actual monarchs such as Elizabeth or James might be expected to present a positive or idealized spectacle of their own royalty through their formal public appearances, playwrights and playing companies could challenge the expectations raised by the sound of a flourish or a sennet in a playhouse context.[15] Thus, *Richard III* never quite gives its audience the display of royal pomp that it repeatedly promises through the musical announcement of formal royal entrance. Frances Ann Shirley has noted the irony that might strike an audience when a royal trumpet call sounds for a king of dubious worth, such as the »pitiful« Henry VI (*3 HVI*, 1.1.206), or the »evil« Richard III (*RIII*, 4.2.0).[16] I would take this idea even further to suggest that by refusing to offer the unequivocal

13 Ibid., pp. 178-182.

14 Stephen Gosson, *Plays Confuted in Five Actions*, London 1582, sig. $E5^r$.

15 It should be noted that, despite such expectations, the reality of appearances by the uncooperative James in particular could range from the underwhelming to the borderline catastrophic. Indeed, Janette Dillon notes that James »was quite open about how repellent he found proximity to his people«. See: Stephen Orgel, »Prologue: I am Richard II«, in: Alessandra Petrina and Laura Tosi (eds.), *Representations of Elizabeth I in Early Modern Culture*, Basingstoke 2011, pp. 11-43 (pp. 30-41); Janette Dillon, *The Language of Space in Court Performance, 1400 – 1625*, Cambridge 2010, p. 45.

16 Shirley (as note 6), p. 73.

and celebratory pageantry that his musical cues anticipate, Shakespeare actually reframes his audience's mode of engagement with the staging of royal spectacle. Instead of being invited to take pleasure in a dazzling visual representation of royalty, early audiences of *Richard III* were instead faced with a series of questions about the appropriate presentation of a monarch, and the characteristics of desirable kingship. By challenging the expectations that the trumpet calls raised in early modern subjects, these moments asked playhouse attendees not just to look, but also to think.

As always with early modern drama, the task of reconstructing musical playhouse practice from the textual record brings challenges. As Tiffany Stern has aptly demonstrated, early printed playbooks are often partial in their recording of music, from missing cues for music that characters are cheerfully discussing, to songs that have disappeared somewhere between playhouse and printing house, leaving only »*Song*« – if anything – in the printed text.[17] Whilst the inclusion of a stage direction in print is thus strong evidence that music *was* heard at a certain point in early performances, the converse lack of any such cue is a far less reliable indicator that music was *not* used. Positive evidence is infinitely more valuable than negative evidence when exploring musical playhouse practices. In the case of *Richard III*, no fewer than ten pre-1642 editions survive. These eight quarto and two folio printings are often, but not always, consistent in the uses of entrance music that they record. A collation of these editions indicates that in relation to musical stage directions, there are two text branches.[18] There are no substantial differences at all in the musical cues of the various quartos, leaving *Q1* (1597) able to stand for this entire branch of eight editions.[19] Likewise, *F2* (1632) is derivative of *F1* (1623), the only change being the excision of trumpet calls for royal exits in the later edition (3.1.149.1; 4.4.469.1). There are therefore just two meaningfully divergent texts in relation to entrance music: *Q1* and *F1*. Frances

17 See: Tiffany Stern, *Documents of Performance in Early Modern England*, Oxford 2009, pp. 120-173.

18 Early quarto and folio editions of *Richard III* are hereafter cited in the text as »*Q1*«, »*Q2*«, »*F1*«, etc. I have collated musical stage directions from quarto editions in the following copies held by the British Library: *Q1* (1597), BL Huth 47; *Q2* (1598), BL C.34.k.47; *Q3* (1602), BL C.34.k.48; *Q4* (1605), BL C.34.k.49; *Q5* (1612), BL C.12.h.10; *Q6* (1622), BL C.34.k.51; *Q7* (1629), BL C.34.k.52; *Q8* (1634), BL C.34.k.63, in: *Treasures of the British Library* <www.bl.uk/treasures/shakespeare/homepage.html> [accessed 5 February 2013]. Folio directions are collated from the Norton *F1* Facsimile (Charlton Hinman and Peter Blayney (eds.), *The First Folio of Shakespeare*, 2. ed., London 1996), and the Methuen & Co. *F2* Facsimile (*Mr William Shakespeare's Comedies, Histories and Tragedies: Faithfully Reproduced in Facsimile from the Edition of 1632*, London 1909).

19 Whilst printing errors do appear, such as the mutation of »the trumpets sound« (*Q2*, 4.4.151) into »The trumepts sounds« (*Q8*, 4.4.151), no new information or detail about music is added in any of the later quartos.

Ann Shirley has remarked of musical stage directions in Shakespearean texts that »[t]he Folio directions are often superior [to Quarto directions] on two counts: frequency and detail«.[20] This is broadly true of *Richard III*. Whilst *Q1* tends towards generalized description of what is heard, such as »*The Trumpets sound*« (4.2.0.1), *F1* instead tends towards specific instructions to a musician, like »*Sound a Sennet*« (4.2.0.1). More marked differences between the texts, however, are the two cases in which *F1* cues a »*Flourish*« for a royal entrance (2.1.0.1; 5.8.0.1), but *Q1* records no music at all. Stanley Wells and Gary Taylor argue that *Q1* is set from a post-performance memorial reconstruction of the play, whilst *F1* draws upon a scribal transcript of the play in a slightly earlier form than that reported in *Q1*, as well as upon later quarto editions, probably *Q3* and *Q6*.[21] It therefore seems likely that *Q1* is simply less consistent and less detailed in its recording of musical cues than *F1*, rather than indicating a different set of performance practices, although this is not certain. I take *F1* to offer the best available account of how music was used in early playhouse performances and follow it throughout, whilst noting where the *F1* text deviates significantly from *Q1*.

The king who reigns at the start of the play, Edward IV, does not appear on stage until the second act. The play instead begins with the unaccompanied entry of an aspirant king: »*Enter Richard, Duke of Gloster, solus*« (1.1.0.1). Next, a former king is represented, when the »*Coarse of Henrie the sixt*« (1.2.0.1) provides the backdrop for Richard's wooing of Lady Anne. These are neither musically accompanied entrances, nor quite spectacles of kingship, although they are scarcely positive precedents for the treatment of royalty in the play. In fact, the first musical cue of any kind does not sound until Edward IV's sole appearance, in 2.1:

> *Flourish.*
> *Enter the King sicke, the Queene, Lord Marquesse*
> *Dorset, Rivers, Hastings, Catesby,*
> *Buckingham, Woodvill.* (2.1.0.1-4)

The stage direction specifies that audience members hear a flourish, and then – no less importantly – see a visibly dying, or »*sicke*«, man.[22] The first royal entrance of the play is thus no dazzling display of pomp, nor even the dignified and commanding entrance of a statesman. Instead, playgoers' expectations following the flourish are confounded directly and deliberately with the sight of a king whose

20 Shirley (as note 6), p. 45.

21 Stanley Wells and Gary Taylor, with John Jowett and William Montgomery, *William Shakespeare: A Textual Companion*, Oxford 1987, pp. 228-232.

22 *Q1* does not record the visual and aural aspects of the scene's opening: »*Enter King, Queene, Hastings, Ryuers, Dorcet, &c.*« (2.1.0.1-3). Besides the lack of music, there is no description of the king's visible sickness, and there are fewer courtiers specified.

corporeal body is failing. Ian Frederick Moulton reads Shakespeare's presentation of Edward through early modern constructions of masculinity, suggesting that his symptoms are »all signs of effeminate weakness of spirit« – Edward is apparently »sickly, weake, and melancholly« (1.1.137).[23] Effeminate or otherwise, weakness is certainly represented in 2.1 through visual means, in this »*sicke*« entrance. Just as the magnificence and splendour of costume at Henry VIII's coronation entry, for instance, constituted a visual performance of royal wealth and power, so would the theatrical sight of Edward's frail, dying body constitute a converse spectacle of weak and ineffective kingship.[24] The line break between the cue for sound and the cue for sight is perhaps more likely to reflect neatness on the part of the *F1* typesetter than anything else, but it nevertheless gives apt emphasis to the two stages of this musical spectacle: first the music sounds, creating distinct expectations, and then these expectations are deliberately subverted through the sight of the king's entry. Playhouse attendees need know nothing of Edward from the preceding scenes, for the contrast between the flourish, signifying formal royal entrance, and the sight of a man close to death would be almost painfully apparent. This is a fundamentally performative means of conveying an abstract notion to an audience: nothing is said; prior knowledge of the characters or their historical counterparts is not necessary; and, critically, it is the actor's body, set against the musician's instrument, that communicates the idea of Edward's weak kingship.

This view of Edward IV is given extensive exposition in the rest of the scene; indeed, the pattern of spectacular statement of kingship followed by dialogic exposition recurs in the play's other musical royal entrances. In this case, the visual representation of a king too physically weak to rule is followed by further exploration of his weakness, through Edward's inability to keep a unified court. Shakespeare amalgamates two historical moments – the 1478 execution of the Duke of Clarence, and Edwards's 1483 deathbed attempts to reconcile the warring court factions of the Woodvilles and Lord Hasting's followers – into a single scene of failed leadership.[25] Edward begins with the upbeat claim that he has »done a good daies work« (2.1.1), proceeding to consolidate the accord that he believes he has negotiated through the school-teacher's traditional – and unconvincing – technique of instructing the quarrelling parties to »take each others hand, / Dissemble not your hatred, Sweare your love« (2.1.7-8). The manifest absurdity of instructing people not just to make gestures of forgiveness and affection, but

23 Ian Frederick Moulton, »›A Monster Great Deformed‹: The Unruly Masculinity of Richard III«, in: *Shakespeare Quarterly* 47 (2006), pp. 251-268 (p. 257).

24 »Costume is the first and most prominent item of display« in Edward Hall's description of Henry's entry. Dillon (as note 15), p. 26.

25 See: Peter Saccio, *Shakespeare's English Kings: History, Chronicle, and Drama*, Oxford 1977, pp. 167-170.

to »do it unfeignedly« is emphasized as the scene unfolds (2.1.22). Richard enters at line forty-four and announces Clarence's death, which Edward had ordered but then reversed. This is Richard's carefully calculated move to exacerbate the factionalism of the court, for as he tells Buckingham at the very end of the scene, the »Kindred of the Queene [...] did urge it [i. e. Clarence's death] still unto the King«, and Edward now holds them partly responsible (2.1.138-139). Next, Stanley's untimely suit asking the king to pardon his servant for killing a man moves Edward to bemoan the self-interestedness of his courtiers, who do not hesitate to ask him to excuse the behaviour of their followers, yet »not a man of you / Had so much grace« as to sue for Clarence's pardon (2.1.120-121). The seeming reconciliation and forgiveness of the preceding shows of friendship now seem bitterly ironic, reflecting poorly both on Edward's capacity to keep his court unified, and his ability even to enact his will, for Clarence is dead against the king's wishes. The sheer helplessness of Edward's final words in the play, »Ah poore *Clarence*« (2.1.135), offer a cogent summary of the kingship explored in the scene: Edward is outmanoeuvred, unable to respond, and ultimately incapable. Notably, this dramatic exposition is concluded with a visual recapitulation of the scene's opening image. Edward instructs Hastings to »helpe me to my Closset« (2.1.134), and with his final, futile apostrophe to his dead brother, the audience are left to watch a dying man as he is assisted from the stage. Shakespeare uses the failing corporeal body of the king to give a concluding visual representation of Edward's failing kingship.

Following this musical spectacle of waning rule, the play's next cue for music introduces a view of kingship that is both embryonic and worryingly detachable from the corporeal body of Edward V:

The Trumpets sound.
Enter yong Prince, the Dukes of Glocester, and Buckingham,
Lord Cardinall, with others. (3.1.0.1-4)

Neither *Q1* nor *F1* specify the particular signal that frames this sight, both stating merely that »*The Trumpets sound*«. Whilst this offers no clue as to whether the sound is a flourish or a sennet, Edward's later exit from the scene to »*A senet*« in *F1* perhaps suggests the latter (3.1.149). Described in this stage direction as »*yo[u]ng Prince*« in all ten early texts, Edward's historical status as a monarch was somewhat complex. In this scene, he is making a formal royal entrance into London in advance of his coronation. He finds himself in the awkward gap between the declaration of his succession, and the ceremonial coronation that will invest him performatively with kingship.[26] Famously, however, Edward did

26 Like royal entrance to a sennet, the coronation ceremony integrated music into the performance of kingship. The *Liber Regalis* describes »The Manner and Form of the King's Corona-

not receive a coronation before he was declared illegitimate and debarred from the throne by act of parliament in 1484. Nonetheless, from the perspective of Shakespeare's early audiences he was certainly a king; Henry VII repealed the 1484 »Titulus Regius« act and ordered all copies of it to be destroyed, whilst the coronation of the sixth Edward in 1547 recognized the earlier »*yong Prince*« as Edward V. Edward is a king in 3.1, but only just, and the musical spectacle that opens the scene conveys precisely this incomplete status. The trumpet sounds to indicate a royal figure arriving, in answer to which the audience is shown a boy. In the previous act, Edward IV's body was fully grown, but irreparably diseased; in 3.1 his son's royal body is healthy, but visibly immature. This is an image of royal potential, but unavoidably one of unripe kingship.

Edward's physical immaturity is not the only problem with the sight that answers the trumpet's call, however. Juvenile rulers such as Henry VI and Edward VI often had a titular ›Lord Protector‹, who would assume many of the duties of the crown in their stead for the duration of the minority. Edward V was no different, and indeed his royal entrance in 3.1 occurs in the immediate company of his Lord Protector: Richard, Duke of Gloucester. In a later scene, Shakespeare explores the problematic fragmentation of royal authority that this situation creates, when Brakenbury, Lieutenant of the Tower, informs Queen Elizabeth that she cannot visit the princes because »[t]he King«, meaning Richard, »hath strictly charg'd the contrary«. When challenged, Brakenbury corrects himself – »I meane, the Lord Protector« – apologizing for his slip in *Q1* but not in *F1*. In response, Elizabeth exclaims, »[t]he Lord protect him from that Kingly Title« (4.1.17-19). Likewise, when the royal entrance in 3.1 presents both minority King and Lord Protector in answer to a single trumpet call, the same problematic separation of Edward's royal body and Richard's presumption of royal power is foregrounded. The format of the stage direction in 3.1 suggests that the pair enter amongst the same party rather than meeting on the stage itself, for elsewhere in the play both *Q1* and *F1* texts give explicit directions for actors to enter separately when a staged meeting is required.[27] The direction organizes the characters by rank, which is likely to reflect the order in which they would have moved onto the stage in this formally announced entrance. Thus, the trumpet call would have been answered by the sight of two almost-kingly figures, with the »*yong Prince*« in front, and the Lord Protector behind him.

tion« in »the Church of Westminster«. The »square Stage« for the ceremony was set »between the Queer [i. e. choir] and the Altar«. Music sung from the choir punctuated proceedings throughout. Dillon notes that the form of this ceremony »was to remain virtually unchanged between c. 1375 and 1685«. *A Collection out of the Book called Liber Regalis*, London 1661, pp. 2 ff.; Dillon (as note 15), p. 36.

27 At 3.7.0.1, for instance, *Q1* notes that »*Glocester* [enters] *at one doore, Buckingham at another*«, whilst *F1* directs the dukes to appear »*at severall Doores*«.

Even in character as Gloucester, Richard Burbage would presumably have been markedly taller than the boy playing Edward, constituting an uncomfortable vision of fractured kingship. The prince's physical form literalizes his unreadiness to rule, whilst Richard's body looming behind or even over him gives a similarly visual realization of the »general division of authority« that a »child monarch« necessitates.[28] This sight, drawing attention to the gap between royal body and royal power, is particularly problematic given the identity of the Lord Protector and his preceding actions in the drama. Shakespeare's interest throughout the play in the relationship between a king's corporeal body and the enacting of royal power is particularly apparent in the literal separation of one from the other in this musically announced entrance.

Just as in the previous act, the opening musical spectacle of Edward V's kingship is explored in detail in the ensuing scene, which once again concludes with a visual recapitulation. In the very first lines, Buckingham emphasizes Edward's juvenility by greeting him as »sweete Prince«, before Richard's address, »Welcome deere Cosin, my thoughts Soveraign«, slyly emphasizes the dispersed royal authority displayed in Edward's entrance (3.1.1-2).[29] E. A. J. Honigmann has noted the »sinister implication« of Richard's mind being focused solely on the young prince, whilst the reference to Edward's sovereignty is itself ironic given Richard's protectorship.[30] Even more unsettling, however, is the pun in this phrase that gestures towards Richard's *de facto* wielding of royal power; this is, after all, the scene in which he boasts of his ability to »morallize two meanings in one word« (3.1.83). Depending on apostrophe placement, the phrase »my thoughts' sovereign« can post-modify »cousin«, indicating that Edward rules Richard's thoughts. However, with different punctuation these three words are a complete sentence of their own, asserting that Richard's desires shall determine what happens: »Welcome cousin. My thought's sovereign.« Both meanings are present when the line is spoken, in another performative complication of Edward's kingship. The lines that follow this ambiguous statement demonstrate both Richard's ostensible, sycophantic adherence to the first meaning, when he deferentially tells Edward that he should reside »where it think'st best unto your Royall self«, and his enacting of the second meaning, as he ensures that Edward nonetheless leaves for the Tower of London, despite his complaint that

28 Moulton (as note 23), p. 256.

29 It is the juvenile sense of »Prince« that Buckingham appears to be emphasizing here, rather than the more general sense of royalty that Elizabeth I alludes to when telling Parliament that »[w]e princes … are set on stages, in the sight and view of all the world duly observed«. Elizabeth I of England, quoted in: J. E. Neale, *Elizabeth I and her Parliaments*, Vol. 2, New York 1958, p. 119.

30 E. A. J. Honigmann (ed.), *Richard III*, The New Penguin Shakespeare, Harmondsworth 1968, 3.1.2n; p. 219.

he »doe[s] not like the Tower, of any place« (3.1.68). Edward is entirely aware that Richard's »counsaile« is not merely advisory; rather, he goes to the Tower because »[m]y Lord Protector [needes] will have it so« (3.1.141).[31] Like his father, Edward V's final exit from the play recapitulates the image of his kingship that his musically announced entrance introduced, this exit image given musical accompaniment in *F1* (3.1.149). As Shirley notes, »[t]he doomed prince, powerless in the hands of his uncle Richard, goes to the Tower with a sennet ringing in his ears«, escorted by Hastings and Dorset.[32] If the trumpet call that opened the scene introduced an ambiguous sight in which royal authority was divided between the young Prince and the Lord Protector, then this cue frames an even gloomier view of Edward's kingship. The sennet draws attention to a royal exit that the king himself does not even want to make; in accordance with Richard's wishes alone, Edward leaves for the Tower with »heavie heart« (3.1.148), offering a concluding, emphatic visual account of the utter separation of royal body and royal authority.

The next royal entrance announced by music, in 4.2, unites exploration of kingship through musical spectacle with the play's other constant presence – Richard himself. I have suggested that trumpet calls for royal entry encountered in other plays would create particular expectations when these sounds appear in *Richard III*. I would argue further that, by the fourth act, audience members' foremost recollections and expectations will be those generated by the royal entrances already performed in the play itself. Twice have the audience heard the announcement of a royal entrance by trumpet, and twice, instead of the vision of royal authority anticipated by this sound, they have been offered the sight of a monarch physically unable to perform powerful kingship. In 4.2, playgoers are finally shown a monarch entering to a sennet with the expected, glamorous trappings of royal spectacle:

> *Sound a Sennet. Enter Richard in pompe, Buckingham, Catesby, Ratcliffe, Lovel.* (4.2.0.1-3)

This time, the contrast is between the ostentatious performance of royalty that follows the sennet, and the dubious claim to kingship of the performer himself. When the sound of the trumpet is finally answered with the sight of Richard »*in pompe*«, unfulfilled expectations from scenes 2.1 and 3.1 now foreground the fervent assertion of royal authority in the grandiose spectacle of 4.2. As John Jowett notes of the scene's possible early staging, »there is opportunity for pageantry here«, and moreover »[i]t is the only moment of its kind in the play«.[33]

31 *Q1* supplies the word, »needes«, which normalizes the scansion of this line (3.1.141).
32 Shirley (as note 6), p. 73.
33 John Jowett (ed.), *Richard III*, The Oxford Shakespeare, Oxford 2000, p. 79.

Yet as the ostentatiousness of this entrance is foregrounded, so is the fact that it is Richard garbed in these trappings of royalty. Significantly, when this entrance occurs, audience members have just been shown Richard's presumptuous self-presentation as a monarch. His kingly self-fashioning in 3.7, as he enters before the Lord Mayor and citizens, is preserved in a precise stage direction for him to appear »*aloft, betweene two Bishops*« (3.7.94.1).[34] By following Buckingham's advice to »stand betweene two Church-men« (3.7.48), Richard presents himself as a monarch being crowned, for the coronation ceremony specifies that the king must enter Westminster Abbey and perform the appropriate rituals »supported [...] by two Bishops«.[35] This visual pastiche of the beginning of the coronation ceremony is recalled two scenes later, when Richard's entrance »*in pompe*« dramatizes the ceremony's conclusion with the king crowned and enthroned. Through this connection to his appearance in 3.7, and through contrast with previous royal entrances, the spectacle of Richard's entrance in 4.2 emphasizes his visual self-fashioning as a king, and his grasping of royal power. This sight introduces two issues returned to throughout 4.2, that of Richard's legitimacy as monarch, and that of the stability of his kingship, given his dubious ascent to the throne. The preceding scenes of royal – and pseudo-royal – entrance (2.1; 3.1; 3.7) thus frame the performance of royalty in Richard's entrance »*in pompe*« as an assertion, rather than a confirmation, of secure monarchical status.

It may seem counter-intuitive to read this moment of musical spectacle in 4.2 not through Richard's body, the site of so much critical attention, but rather through his pompous attire.[36] However, I suggest that this reflects the priorities of the *F1* text. Each of the musical stage directions that I have con-

34 *Q1* notes the format of this entrance rather untidily: »*Enter Rich with two bishops aloste* [*sic*]« (3.7.94.1).

35 *Liber Regalis* (as note 26), pp. 4-5. See: Siemon (as note 5), 3.7.93.1n; p. 297.

36 Recent work on Richard's body includes: Mark Thornton Burnett, »›Monsters‹ and ›Molas‹: Body Politics in *Richard III*«, in: *Constructing Monsters in Shakespearean Drama and Early Modern Culture*, Basingstoke 2002, pp. 65-94; Marjorie Garber, »Descanting on Deformity: Richard III and the Shape of History«, in: *Shakespeare's Ghost Writers: Literature as Uncanny Causality*, 2. ed., Abingdon 2010, pp. 37-68; Robert McRuer, »Fuck the Disabled: The Prequel«, in: Madhavi Menon (ed.), *Shakesqueer: A Queer Companion to the Complete Works of Shakespeare*, Durham 2011, pp. 294-301; David T. Mitchell and Sharon L. Snyder, »Performing Deformity: The Making and Unmaking of Richard III«, in: *Narrative Prosthesis: Disability and the Dependencies of Discourse*, Ann Arbor, MI 2000, pp. 95-118; Moulton (as note 23); Katherine Schaap, »Enabling Richard: The Rhetoric of Disability in *Richard III*«, in: *Disability Studies Quarterly* 29 (2009) [no pagination]. Fittingly, the writing of this article on Shakespeare's Richard has coincided precisely with the University of Leicester's announcement that the skeleton excavated in 2012 from a Leicester City Council car park is indeed that of the historical king. See: *The Search for Richard III – Completed* <http://www.le.ac.uk/richardiii> [accessed 8 February 2013].

sidered encompasses three pieces of information: the characters who need to enter, a musical cue, and a visual description of the entering king. Edward IV is »*sicke*«, Edward V »*yong*«, and Richard »*in pompe*«. It is the clothes and other finery that Richard wears that are identified as the key visual element of this entrance. The stage direction does not draw attention to the form of Richard's body as a key element of this sight, although admittedly one could argue that this needs no textual annotation. There is perhaps a corporeal emphasis to the lines immediately following, when Richard instructs Buckingham to »Give me thy hand« as he mounts the throne (4.2.3). However, it is unclear in the early printed texts whether he does this out of physical necessity – as many later productions have explored – or simply to signify his recognition of Buckingham's role in his assumption of power, as indeed his next line verbalizes: »Thus high, by thy advice, and thy assistance, / Is King *Richard* seated« (4.2.4-5).[37] At least in his musically announced royal entrance, Richard's kingship emerges in the gap between the image of royal authority that his vestments seek to project, and his actual monarchical status, rather than in the form of his body.[38]

The scene that follows Richard's spectacular entrance continues to draw attention to his grasping of the crown, and to the instability created by his assumption of power. Shakespeare once again amalgamates and augments episodes from chronicle sources in order to facilitate this exploration of Richard's kingship.[39] Immediately upon announcing that he is now »seated« as king, Richard asks Buckingham whether he will only »weare these Glories for a day?« (4.2.6). Within a few lines, he names one threat that concerns him: »Young *Edward* lives« (4.2.11). Indeed, Richard vocalizes unease about the danger to his kingship both from the young princes and from Henry Richmond throughout the scene, even whilst plotting strategic murders to consolidate his position. He seeks to eliminate both Edward IV's yet-living sons and his own wife Anne, in the latter case so he can »be marryed to my Brothers Daughter« and thus strengthen his claim to the throne (4.2.62). Yet just as the pomp of his state entrance appears not as the embodiment of royal authority but rather as the grasping of power, so do these extreme gestures of violence appear increasingly desperate as noble

37 Jowett (as note 33), 4.2.1-3n; pp. 285-286.

38 Richard's tongue-in-cheek remarks in 1.1 do construct a set of relationships between his body and his actions in the play. However, he does not mention kingship, or even a desire for power, in this context. Rather, he explains that whilst he enjoys the violence of war, he is unsuited to peacetime because his body is »curtail'd of this faire Proportion« necessary to »prove a Lover«. His »plots« against his brothers are framed as an alternative source of amusement to the »idle pleasures« that he is excluded from because of his physical appearance (1.1.18-32). His body is thus invoked as the cause of his behaviour, rather than the manifestation of his personal or kingly qualities.

39 Saccio (as note 25), p. 176-177.

support ebbs from Richard. His pointed remark to Buckingham regarding the princes – »I wish the Bastards dead« (4.2.19) – falls on deaf ears; the scene ends with Buckingham leaving both the court and Richard.[40] Likewise, even as Richard summons Sir James Tyrrell to arrange the princes' murders, Lord Stanley enters and announces that »*Dorset* [...] is fled to *Richmond*« (4.2.49-50). This ebbing of support is recapitulated in the scene's final visual statement. Richard's refusal to grant Buckingham »[t]h'Earldome of Hertford« culminates in the two parting upon the stage, Richard exiting first (presumably with the remainder of the court in attendance), whilst Buckingham remains on the stage, expressing regret at having »made [...] him King« and resolving to retire »to Brecnock, while my fearefull Head is on« (4.2.93-125).[41] The scene closes with a visual account of Richard's increasingly precarious kingship, in his literal separation from his closest ally.

Before reaching the fourth musically announced royal entrance of the play, there are two scenes that present the rather different sights and sounds of military marching music, first for Richard, and then for Henry Richmond. In both cases they are marching to war. *Q1* is explicit that Richard enters »marching with Drummes and Trumpets« in 4.4, whilst in *F1*, Richard's reference to his drums and trumpets as »the clamorous report of Warre« makes clear that his »Expedition« in this scene is martial (4.4.135-153). Likewise, Richmond reminds his »Fellowes in Armes« that they have »marcht on without impediment« when he enters in 5.2, with »drum and colours« in *F1* and with »drums and trumpets« in *Q1* (5.2.1-4). Of the known trumpet calls, the tucket would be appropriate to accompany these entrances, for as Markham notes, in a military context this call signifies »Marching after the Leader« (I3^r^). This convention was followed in playhouse practice; indeed, the 1592 printing of Thomas Kyd's *The Spanish Tragedy* cues »*A tucket a farre off*«, which is obligingly glossed for the King by his General: »This tels me that your graces men of warre, / [...] Come marching on towards your royall seate« (1.2.99-104).[42] These moments are therefore likely to have sounded distinct from the flourishes and sennets announcing royalty, as indeed the accompanying sight of military marching is visually distinct from the play's earlier royal entries. These marches signify a shift in dramatic register from peace to war. Moreover, in the case of Richmond, his entrance to military music in 5.2 prefigures the final scene, 5.8, in which a flourish will finally announce his entrance with the crown.

40 *F1* does not indicate this scene break, but the stage is cleared by Buckingham's exit before Tyrrell enters. See: Jowett (as note 33), 4.2.125; p. 293.

41 »Brecnock« (i. e. Brecon) was »Buckingham's stronghold in south Wales«. Jowett (as note 33), 4.2.124n; p. 293.

42 Thomas Kyd, *The Spanish Tragedie*, London 1592, sig. A4^v^. Line reference keyed to: Katharine Eisaman Maus (ed.), »The Spanish Tragedy«, in: *Four Revenge Tragedies*, Oxford 1995, pp. 1-92.

Notably, the title page of *F1* highlights just two specific events in the play: »the Landing of Earle Richmond« (5.2), and »the Battell at Bosworth Field« (5.5-8). The former begins with Richmond marching onstage to military drum, whilst the latter is concluded with his musically announced entrance to be crowned as Henry VII:

> *Retreat, and Flourish. Enter Richmond, Derby bearing the Crowne, with divers other Lords.* (5.8.0.3-6)

Functionally, this is a coronation scene. Announced by a trumpet, Richmond enters with the crown borne behind him, speaks to the assembled lords, and ceremonially accepts the crown from Lord Stanley, Earl of Derby with a prayer – »Great God of Heaven, say Amen to all« (5.8.0-8).[43] Yet the long-established conventions of the English coronation ceremony are missing: this is not Westminster, but a battlefield; there is no choir present to sing hymns where appropriate; and, perhaps most noticeably, Henry is not in pomp, but in armour.[44] The military elements of the scene in fact complicate the entrance further by adding a second signification to the sound of the trumpet flourish. As well as announcing royal entrances, flourishes were conventionally used in early modern playhouse performance to indicate victory in a battle. A particularly explicit cue for »A Long charge after a Flourish for Victory« in Philip Massinger's *The Maid of Honour* demonstrates this signification.[45] As David Lindley notes, the final flourish in *Richard III* is a »royal salute to the victorious Richmond«.[46] Thus, two contrasting versions of idealized kingship are evoked simultaneously in Henry's entrance: the humility and piety performed in the coronation ceremony, and the strength and might displayed by a victorious martial leader. Even in this performance of more encouraging royal spectacle, the play reminds its audience that there is more than one way to think about kingship, even in idealized terms. Shakespeare once again challenges the possibility of an uncritical playhouse response to the representation of royalty.

Indeed, the fact that the coronation entrance occurs on a battlefield draws attention to the means by which Richmond has secured the throne. Mark Thornton Burnett has argued that »[b]ecause a true ›line‹ is restored in the ›lineaments‹ of Richmond and Elizabeth of York, two possibilities are avoided – the ›monsterization‹ of the nation, and the ascension to the throne of a ›monstrous‹

43 This final trumpet call is absent from *Q1*, which describes the »*retrait being sounded*« after Richard is slain, but no flourish for Richmond's re-entry to be crowned (5.8.0.1-6).

44 In the coronation ceremony at Westminster, whilst monarchs disrobed for the anointing of their body, they were »robed for the coronation itself and crowned […] by the Archbishop of Canterbury«. Dillon (as note 15), p. 42; *Liber Regalis* (as note 26).

45 Philip Massinger, *The Maid of Honour*, London 1632, sig. E3^{v}.

46 Lindley (as note 1), p. 117.

interloper«.[47] This final musically announced sight of royalty certainly presents Henry as an infinitely preferable monarch to Richard. However, it is not true that the *possibility* of Richard's ascension is avoided, for some ten scenes earlier, a sennet announced Richard's royal entrance to mount his throne (4.2.0.1-3). Herein lies the difficulty of this final entrance: in recovering the crown from a regicidal interloper, Richmond has had to commit regicide and become a usurper himself. Of the historical monarch, Stephen Orgel notes that »Henry reigned without even a doubtful claim to the English throne«, and did so »only after the deposition and execution of a reigning claimant whose pedigree was, unlike [Richmond's], impeccable«.[48] This problem is embodied in the musical spectacle of 5.8 by the one character who, I suggest, is already onstage when Richmond makes his entrance – Richard himself. There is a wider textual difficulty here in how the crown gets from Richard's on-stage head at 5.8.0.2-3 to Stanley's off-stage hands when he enters »*bearing the Crowne*« at 5.8.0.4-5. Yet however this is resolved, I argue that Richard's body should remain on stage, for it serves as a visible prop when Stanley indicates »*this* bloudy Wretch« a few lines into the scene (5.8.5; my emphasis).[49] If early performances indeed kept Richard on the stage, then the complexity of the sight that answered the play's final musical cue was substantial. Henry enters to be crowned as king, passing the body of the monarch who he has just killed in order to achieve this advancement. Indeed, Stanley's aforementioned reference to »the dead Temples of this bloudy Wretch« as he is crowning Richmond draws attention to the corporeal stage presence, even as the coronation scene unfolds (5.8.5). Undoubtedly, Richmond's action would have been understood by early playhouse audiences as a positive regicide, presumably evoking responses in keeping with the *Q1* title page's reference to Richard's »most deserved death«.[50] Yet just as the over-assertiveness of this 1597 paratext demonstrates that the events of the play need careful justification if they

47 Burnett (as note 36), p. 90.

48 Stephen Orgel, »The Spectacles of State«, in: Richard C. Trextler (ed.), *Persons in Groups: Social Behavior as Identity Formation in Medieval and Renaissance Europe*, Binghamton, NY 1985, pp. 101-122 (pp. 109-117).

49 See: Wells and Taylor (as note 21), p. 249. Immediately prior to Richmond's spectacular entrance, »*Richard / is slaine*« on the stage in a skirmish specifying the stage presence only of »*Richard and Richmond*« (5.8.0.1-3), yet in the very next direction, Stanley must enter already »*bearing the / Crowne*« which, he announces pointedly, he has just »pluck'd off« Richard's »dead Temples« (5.8.5-6). Both of the two crown-moving solutions suggested by Wells and Taylor require slight emendation of the *F1* text. Following one suggestion, if Stanley only »pick[s] it up as he enters and moves towards Richmond«, then he does not quite »*Enter* [...] *bearing the / Crowne*«. Alternatively, if Richmond »drag[s] off the body« after the fight then Stanley can collect the crown in the tiring house before entering, but he is left to gesture vaguely towards an absent corpse at 5.8.5.

50 *Q1*, sig. A1^{r}.

are to appear acceptable, so too does the stagecraft of this moment of musical spectacle insist upon raising questions, even in moments of positivity. A trumpet flourish is finally answered with the sight of a competent and strong leader, yet through Henry's military garb and the stage presence of a royal corpse, playhouse attendees not only face two competing sets of musical signification, but are also given a final visual reminder of the questionable means through which Richmond has arrived at the crown. Even in a celebratory moment, Shakespeare ensures that *Richard III*'s concluding spectacle of kingship is neither completely idealized nor entirely straightforward.

In early playhouse performances, *Richard III* offered views of royalty radically distinct from those expected when Elizabeth or James made formal public appearances. In the play, the sights that follow flourishes and sennets repeatedly emphasize the gap between abstract ideals of kingship, and the embodied reality of actual monarchs. These musical spectacles of royal entrance were central to the early performance impact of this self-consciously theatrical play, at the heart of how playwright and playing company sought to communicate with their playhouse audiences. Indeed, we can think about these moments of spectacle in *Richard III* in two ways. Immediately, they each make an important local contribution to the portrayal of a particular king, introducing views of Edward IV, Edward V, Richard III and Henry VII that are then developed in the ensuing scene. Yet simultaneously, these moments are distinct from the rest of the drama. In a play that makes precise use of music, these four memorable combinations of trumpet call and visual challenging of expectation would stand out, forming a continuous exploration of kingship that punctuates the entire performance. Instead of offering an unequivocally glorious sight to revel in, these regularly placed moments of theatrical spectacle keep drawing the audience's attention back to the question of what a desirable monarch, or good kingship, might look like. Through sights of a dying man, a boy, Richard's pomp and Henry's martial coronation over Richard's body, the play offered its early theatrical audiences views of kingship that were never idealized, always corporeally manifested, and counter to expectations. This might help us think of early performances of the play that were not entirely dominated by Richard, if this exploration of kingship through four different monarchs provided a significant counterpoint to Richard Burbage's renowned portrayal of his Plantagenet namesake.

The trumpet calls of *Richard III* perhaps even offer some wider suggestions about the relationships between playwrights, playhouses and music in early modern culture. Shakespeare emerges from this enquiry as a playwright deliberately shaping playhouse response through precise use of musical sounds and their cultural resonances. Recent work by Elizabeth Ketterer on music in the repertory of the Admiral's Men demonstrates the substantial insight to be gained from interrogating the music of early modern drama through the cultural and material specificities of the early modern theatre industry, and *Richard III* confirms that a playwright's musical intentions can be illuminated productively through reference to playhouse performance.[51] Intriguingly, *Richard III* suggests further that dramatically subtle use of playhouse music is not necessarily synonymous with extensive instrumental resources, or even with sophisticated music. The play does not require complex harmony, yet its drums and trumpets fulfil extremely sophisticated dramatic functions. Even without song, dance, masque, or elaborate instrumental music, *Richard III* had the musical resources of the early modern playhouse at the centre of its dramaturgical intentions. Finally, a performance-orientated account of dramatic music requires a focus not just on the playwright, but also on playhouse audiences and their cultural encounters with music. Recent studies by Bruce R. Smith and Christopher Marsh have transformed our understanding of the wider cultural resonances of music in early modern England, with the playhouse emerging as a significant social space in this picture.[52] The example of *Richard III* suggests that by considering how early modern subjects might respond to music in the playhouse, we can find new insights into dramatic texts and performances.

51 Elizabeth Ketterer, »›Govern'd by Stops, Aw'd by Dividing Notes‹: The Functions of Music in the Extant Repertory of the Admiral's Men, 1594 – 1621« (unpublished doctoral thesis, University of Birmingham 2009) <http://etheses.bham.ac.uk/352/> [accessed 31 July 2012].

52 Smith, *Acoustic World* (as note 1); Christopher Marsh, *Music and Society in Early Modern England*, Cambridge 2010.

Galena Hashhozheva

The Mousetrap

A Court Spectacle and Its Jurisdictions

The city tragedians' performance of »The Murder of Gonzago« and its introduction by a dumb show in *Hamlet* constitute one of the most celebrated examples of the play-within-the-play device in the corpus of Renaissance drama. Hamlet's plan to obtain evidence of Claudius' guilt occasions a structurally complicated scene in which the spectators of *Hamlet* watch how the prince watches Claudius watching the players before him and simultaneously, in his mind's eye, watching himself murder the old king when the parallel incident in the Gonzago play prompts Claudius' involuntary memory. In a separate and no less important chain, spectators watch how Claudius and the entire court watch Hamlet watching and reacting energetically to the »Murder of Gonzago«, since all other characters – as victims of Hamlet's misbehaviour – are anxious to discover whether his ostensibly conciliatory initiative to organize a courtly entertainment and to forget his melancholy will hold, or else will break down into yet another of his vexing tricks. With each step, the recursive pattern of spectation appears to reach deeper and deeper into the private realm where each consciousness is sovereign and sovereignly endeavours to keep itself inviolable. Whether a consciousness is guilty, like that of Claudius, or untainted, as Hamlet's, the gazes that pry into it to the accompaniment of a popular tragedy commit an offense. The intent watching, cued by the hackneyed theatrical scenes, is as obscene and penetrative as Hamlet's lewd remarks on the occasion of the performance and his equally lewd move of sitting at Ophelia's feet and putting his head between her legs (3.2.113).[1] In the crossfire of searching gazes, everyone's soul feels as though it were a violated Ophelia – violated because examined by unauthorized eyes.

Fully authorized to pry into souls' matters are, of course, the eyes of God. In discussing the phenomenon of inwardness in drama, Katharine Eisaman Maus points out that »inwardness in the English Renaissance is almost always formulated in terms of a double spectatorship« – by the omniscient God, before whom all hearts lie open, and by a »limited, fallible human observer« to whom

1 All quotations from *Hamlet* follow the Arden edition, ed. Harold Jenkins, London 1982.

the hearts of his fellow beings normally appear as enigmas.[2] Yet a human observer can begin to bridge the knowledge gap between himself and God by witnessing and contemplating the limited observational capacities of others.[3] One who stands at several removes from the original object of interest, with several more limited observers in between, can see more, including the others' fallacies and naiveté, and gain advantage over them. The audience of *Hamlet* is thus in a position to come closest to God's omniscience. But in the play, Hamlet himself is the most privileged observer among those who are endowed merely with a mortal erring sight. In orchestrating a theatrical Mousetrap, he aims to force the inwardness of Claudius' soul out into the externalized medium of the stage and to play with it as it suits him, as though it were a mouse in the paws of a cat. Crystallized in the statement »The play's the thing / Wherein I'll catch the conscience of the King« (2.2.600-601), Hamlet's resolution reifies the play as well as the king and his conscience, rendering all three as controllable as things are. In the wake of the Mousetrap, Hamlet explicitly ascribes this quality of thing-ness to the King in response to Rosencrantz and Guildenstern's inquiries as to the whereabouts of Polonius' corpse:

> ROSENCRANTZ. My lord, you must tell us where the body is and go with us to the King.
> HAMLET. The body is with the King, but the King is not with the body. The King is a thing –
> GUILDENSTERN. A thing, my lord? (4.3.24-27)

Through the Mousetrap, Hamlet desires to reach a knowledge more true and an interpretation of Danish court affairs more complete than those of any other character. Insofar as Hamlet's starting point in his theatrical stratagem is the story of the ghost, the Mousetrap tests not only the assumption about Claudius' guilt but also the ghost's veracity as an informer. Part of Hamlet's ambition is thus to gain the upper hand even over the ghost, a supernatural authority possessed of a higher knowledge. Hamlet becomes increasingly manipulative and sadistic, crosses boundaries of decorum, and oversteps jurisdictions to which, at best, he has a tenuous claim. With a cold cruelty, he dissects the relations between the living and the dead of Elsinore by means of an artfully arranged public spectacle in a charged courtly milieu. In effect both art and justice, and their codified systems, suffer the incursions of this grim investigator. He avails himself of an unfair license and takes liberties with legal principles and parameters of artistic propriety. To engineer the Mousetrap and to ensure its success as a highly struc-

2 Katharine Eisaman Maus, »Proof and Consequences: Inwardness and its Exposure in the English Renaissance«, in: *Representations* 34 (1991) spring, p. 38.
3 Ibid.

tured experiment, Hamlet mobilizes the resources of these two domains – art and justice – only to abuse and compromise them in the pursuit of a goal alien to them: a warrant for the murder of Claudius.

1. The instrumentalization of art

Hamlet seems to have always nourished a keen interest in dramatic art. He is on familiar terms with the city players, knows by heart passages from their repertoire (2.2.444-62), and understands the theatre business well enough to gossip about its vicissitudes (2.2.326-64). Most impressively, Hamlet can discourse in an eloquent, opinionated manner about dramatic art while instructing the players in their own profession. Ultimately, Hamlet's knowledge of drama and its potential allows him to ghost-direct »The Murder of Gonzago« and even to make his own addition – the key speech of the murderer Lucianus – to an apparently well-established playtext based on an original written, as Hamlet himself can judge, »in very choice Italian« (3.2.256-57).[4] For the melancholy prince, the play becomes like an art project, which he intends to polish with full confidence in his aesthetic acumen.

Before the Mousetrap, when Hamlet gives the players various technical injunctions, it may appear that he does so out of a commitment to drama and its advancement, without any hint of ulterior motives. For example, he recommends an acting style that does not »o'erstep [...] the modesty of nature« (3.2.19), that is, a style that has emotional power but still remains unexaggerated. This emphasis on verisimilitude and naturalism usually earns praise from Shakespearean scholars, for whom Hamlet's instructions reflect the author's own theory of theatre, of what works and what does not work on stage.[5] Yet it will be gradually revealed that Hamlet's aesthetic choices serve a purpose that has nothing to do with art. During the Mousetrap, as the actual performance begins to deviate from

4 On the question whether there is really enough evidence for us to identify any passage from the Mousetrap as the »speech of some dozen or sixteen lines« (2.2.535) that Hamlet has warned the players that he would like to insert in »The Murder of Gonzago«, see Jenkins (as note 1), pp. 481-482, who is unnecessarily dogmatic. The speech of the poisoner Lucianus (3.2.249-54), although it is only six lines in length, is the best candidate because it is at this speech that Claudius calls for the lights. Hamlet's insistent references to »one speech« (»if his occulted guilt / Do not itself unkennel in one speech«, 3.2.80-81) and »the talk of poisoning« (3.2.283), while discussing, first his expectations, and after the Mousetrap, his observations of what happened during the performance, suggest that what Claudius ended up reacting to was precisely what Hamlet added ingeniously as an especial bait, which included the poisoning theme. That explains how Hamlet can feel so triumphant.

5 For an example of an extended discussion of Hamlet's dramatic aesthetic, see Nigel Alexander, *Poison, Play, and Duel*, London 1971, pp. 91-118.

Hamlet's express guidelines, his growing exasperation, culminating in his direct violation of the illusionist barrier between stage and audience, suggests that his real objective in giving those guidelines was something other than a concern for mimetic decorum and verisimilitude. At first Hamlet addresses his critical remarks about the actors' infelicitous choices to the other courtiers who are watching the Mousetrap. With the poisoner's entry, however, Hamlet's relative restraint evaporates, and the prince explodes into a surly command shot for the first time directly at the stage: »Begin, murderer. Leave thy damnable faces and begin« (3.2.246-47). With this interruption Hamlets descends to the level of Polonius, whose awkward prompts and criticisms punctuated an earlier dramatic performance that one of the players gave for Hamlet's personal delectation. Like Hamlet, who cues the Mousetrap's murderer to cut a long superfluous scene, Polonius tried to curtail and tame the player's delivery with interventions such as »This is too long« (2.2.494) and »Prithee no more« (2.2.516). Back then Hamlet reacted by silencing the *senex* with abusive threats to the effect that if he continues complaining about the length of the actor's speech, his long old beard will suffer: »It shall to the barber's with your beard« (2.2.495). Unlike Polonius, however, Hamlet has a reason other than an ignoramus' impatience with art when he demands that the Mousetrap actor stop his grimacing. The timing of Hamlet's demand is significant: the entry of Lucianus is the one scene in the Mousetrap that has the greatest potential to trigger Claudius' self-betrayal. Given the importance of the scene, it must steer clear of overdone grimacing and posturing if it aims to cause Claudius an earnest and unbearable perturbation that he will be unable to hide, rather than laughter or a similar reaction of relief.

Embarrassingly, Hamlet shares his interested endorsement of verisimilitude once again with Polonius. The nunnery scene, which immediately precedes the scene of Hamlet's instructions to the players, opens with Polonius »directing« Ophelia how to play the part of a dignified maid who is entitled to seek explanations from her suitor for his puzzling erratic behaviour. Since this is not a reflection of how Ophelia would act if left to her own devices, Polonius has to erase any traces of pretence in this scene with which he and Claudius are preparing to fool Hamlet. Polonius demands realism and plausibility: »Ophelia, walk you here [...] Read on this book, / That show of such an exercise may colour / Your loneliness« (3.1.43-46). Considering how intensive Ophelia's supervision by her family usually is, Polonius fears with good reason that her »loneliness« in this moment may appear unnatural and hence suspicious. Despite Polonius' directing efforts, however, once Hamlet joins in, the scene veers off the prescribed track and provokes a brutal ›realism‹ that the old man could not have imagined.

Since in the sequence of the action we come to Hamlet's defence of verisimilitude (3.2) after its abuse by the awkward Polonius (3.1), Hamlet's theories and guidelines are thereby discredited in advance. Indeed, in Polonius' shadow they even begin to sound Polonian. Suspiciously circumstantial, Hamlet's lecture on drama is delivered with an excess of examples and restatements of the same points: »you must acquire and beget a *temperance*« (3.2.7) is similar to »that you o'erstep not the *modesty*« (3.2.19); »o'erdoing Termagant« is too much like the »out-Herod«-ing of Herod (3.2.13-14); and the concern that infelicitous choices may »make the unskillful laugh« (3.2.25) reappears in the reproach of clowns who »will themselves laugh, to set on some quantity of barren spectators to laugh too« (3.2.40-41). Hamlet's aggressive insistence betrays the real stake of his theories, which goes beyond a concern for art. All along he has been thinking of one thing: that he needs realistic acting for his stratagem against Claudius to bear fruit. Hamlet is motivated by exigency rather than artistic freedom.

In an age that celebrated the capacity of drama, and literature generally, to teach and delight, this overly instrumental use of the Mousetrap in *Hamlet* poses a problem. Hamlet purposes not only to stir certain emotions in Claudius through the play, but also to isolate those emotions from the volatile and ambiguous aesthetic conditions in which they were generated and to treat them as hard, unequivocal evidence. The framework of art and realistic mimesis is offered and Claudius is invited to react, but his reaction is then moved out of that framework and into reality. Thus neither Claudius nor art wins, and the twin impact of delight and moral improvement cannot take place because the bond between the play and its spectator is compromised by the intervention of an interested third party. In a similar way, Hamlet has previously insinuated himself and his detective purpose into the creative dynamic between the artists and their performance. It is little wonder that Hamlet finds fault with the Mousetrap while the performance is underway, with so many details passing before his eyes, to which his goal-oriented design has originally assigned a different focus, intonation, or look. Yet Hamlet's dissatisfaction is unfair. In his instrumental misuse of art, Hamlet denies the players their wonted license while at the same time claiming for himself too much license in an art that he does not professionally know or practice.

Hamlet's lack of respect for art's principles can be formulated as a problem of jurisdiction and its violations. Ironically, several key features of Hamlet's own theory of drama place him within an intellectual tradition that acknowledges the status of poetry, including dramatic poetry, as a domain with its own canons and protocols, and its own formal and final causes. This tradition begins with Aristotle, who wrote the *Poetics* in a complex dialogue with Plato, and flows into sixteenth-century literary criticism. Already in the opening of his treatise, Aristotle presents poetics as a special field of inquiry studying an autonomous art – poetry – that ought to be both practiced in accordance with its own intrinsic principles and judged in its own terms. Hamlet speaks in an Aristotelian vein when he commends mimetic art for holding »the mirror up to nature« (3.2.22), when he argues that through »temperance« (3.2.7) the actors should find a golden mean between being too »tame« (3.2.16) and too »robustious« (3.2.9), and when he advises against sensationalist spectacle for its own sake, for instance in the form of »inexplicable dumb-shows and noise« (3.2.12).[6] Hamlet's critical discourse on drama resembles that of Aristotle also in its combination of description, whereby Hamlet surveys the current practice of city companies he knows, and prescription, which he utters in a rather peremptory voice. Yet although Hamlet sounds Aristotelian, oddly enough he does not honour the self-determination and *telos* to which the art of drama should be entitled. Hamlet stretches his jurisdiction within the domain of drama from that of a sympathetic patron and recipient to an exploiter. The outcome of the Mousetrap, which fully satisfies Hamlet, would not satisfy Aristotle. The performance is suspended halfway through the plot, and thus one of the fundamental conventions of drama – the relief and purgation of intense emotions provoked by the plot as a logical whole – remains unrealized. Instead of being purged, Claudius' soul boils over, for Hamlet has designed the play in such a way as to add to rather than to reduce the superfluity of passion and corruption that already surfeits the king on account of his own crimes. The Aristotelian catharsis has neglected Claudius:

> GUILDENSTERN. [the King] Is in his retirement marvelous distempered.
> HAMLET. With drink, sir?
> GUILDENSTERN. No, my lord, with choler.
> HAMLET. Your wisdom should show itself more richer to signify this to the doctor, for for me to put him to his purgation would perhaps plunge him into more choler. (3.2.293-299)

Claudius imbibes the play's added dose of abomination even in its verbal form. The epithet »rank«, for example, wanders from the stage murderer's apostrophe to his poison as »Thou mixture rank« (3.2.251) into Claudius' litany of self-pity and self-abasement in the prayer scene: »O, my offense is rank, it smells to heaven« (3.3.36). Clearly, Hamlet's play has ignored drama's principled commitment to catharsis and has poured vile miasma into Claudius' ear and conscience.

Hamlet's understanding of the nature of drama, however, is not exhausted with the quasi-Aristotelianism – marked by its emphasis on decorous mimesis –

6 Aristotle warns against excess and overemphasis on spectacle in *Poetics*, trs. Stephen Halliwell, Cambridge, MA 1995, 1453b: »Those who use spectacle to create an effect not of the fearful but only of the sensational have nothing at all in common with tragedy, as it is not every pleasure that one should seek from tragedy, but the appropriate kind.«

that he propounds in front of the players. Hamlet is also fascinated with certain elements from the antithetical Platonic theory of poetic fury and the transference of poetry's magnetic power to the audience (2.2.544-560; 584-593). For Aristotle poetry, including dramatic poetry, is a *technē*, that is, a field ruled by the artist's knowledge and rational skill. Hamlet's coaching of the players makes sense only if Hamlet assumes their power of choice to perform in one way rather than another and to work in a spirit of selectivity rather than necessity. That is why Hamlet can also insist that they should exercise their »discretion« (3.2.16), which implies judgment and discrimination between different possibilities. His further demands that the players' physical comportment be steeped in a certain »smoothness« (3.2.8) and their speeches delivered »trippingly on the tongue« (3.2.2) likewise build on the Aristotelian conception of drama as a *technē* and more precisely, as a synergy of perfectible techniques. For their perfection artists bear the sole responsibility, since their practice is within their conscious control. Yet such Aristotelian assumptions about the artists' rational control have already been cast in some dubiety before Hamlet's coaching of the players. At the company's entry in 2.2, the chief player – as yet untutored in Hamlet's theory of dramatic *technē* – treats us to a stunning delivery of a passage about the climax of the Trojan War. So extreme is the player's inspiration and so real his emotion even in its physical symptoms, that Polonius, discomfited, comments: »Look whe'er he has not turned his colour and has tears in's eyes« (2.2.515-16). The player's tears and overall state of transport are reminiscent of the condition of the Homeric rhapsode in Plato's *Ion*.[7] The Renaissance knew the *Ion* for Socrates' thesis that poets, rhapsodes, and actors have no rational control over their poetry, or over themselves for that matter, while composing or performing, since they are as it were possessed by a *daimon*. The inspiring force causes them to feel overwhelmed with emotion and even to cry during their recitals. Ion certainly undergoes this ecstasy when performing the choicest Homeric passages, for example a passage that – like the Trojan scene recited by the player in *Hamlet* – concerns Priam and Hecuba.[8] Hamlet's evaluation of the transport of dramatic performers is complex and contradictory:

> Is it not monstrous that this player here,
> But in a fiction, in a dream of passion,
> Could force his soul so to his own conceit
> That from her working all his visage wann'd,

7 Plato, *Ion*, trs. W. R. M. Lamb, in *Plato In Twelve Volumes*, Vol. 8, Cambridge, MA 1975, 535c-d. Shakespeare may have been familiar with the ideas of the *Ion* via their transmission in the Renaissance.

8 Ibid., 535b.

Tears in his eyes, distraction in his aspect,
A broken voice, and his whole function suiting
With forms to his conceit? And all for nothing!
For Hecuba!
What's Hecuba to him, or he to her,
That he should weep for her? What would he do
Had he the motive and the cue for passion
That I have? He would drown the stage with tears,
And cleave the general ear with horrid speech,
Make mad the guilty and appall the free,
Confound the ignorant, and amaze indeed
The very faculties of eyes and ears. (2.2.545-560)

Hamlet's attention to the psycho-physiological symptoms that dramatic performance generates is Platonic in spirit. Like Socrates, Hamlet is interested in the paradoxical phenomenon of a performer developing a storm of passion in the absence of a real cause. Hamlet's rhetorical question »What's Hecuba to him, or he to her, / That he should weep for her?« and the exclamation »And all for nothing!« are paralleled by Socrates' bewildered interrogations of Ion: why should, for instance, Ion's hair stand on end with fear during recitations of fearful passages, when he is »before more than twenty thousand friendly people, none of whom is stripping him or injuring him« or giving him any other grounds for fear?[9] Yet unlike Socrates, Hamlet refrains from hypothesizing that the performer's deep emotional immersion, to the point of self-oblivion, in his performed material may be due to some supernatural force taking possession of him. From his encounter with his father's ghost, Hamlet knows too well what real supernaturalism looks like. What remains, then, is the Aristotelian solution of attributing the performer's emotions to his mastery of mimesis and simulation. As Hamlet puts it, the actor's ostensible transport is an effect of his consciously »forc[ing] his soul« and discriminatingly »suiting« his entire bodily presence »to his own conceit«, that is, to a »fiction«. Indeed, Hamlet proceeds to speculate about what a great difference it would make if the player felt real, not artificially induced, emotions that arise from an authentic »motive« such as a parent's death. Hamlet's conjecture is that such authenticity would have an especial impact on the artist's audience: »He would [...] Make mad the guilty and appall the free, / Confound the ignorant, and amaze indeed / The very faculties of eyes and ears.«

But with this comment Hamlet is back to Platonic allusions. In the *Ion* Socrates argues for a direct chain of causation from the sublimity of the poet's inspiration, to the intensity of the performer's delivery, and finally to the enthrallment of the

9 Ibid., 535d.

spectator. Like a Magnesian stone, poetry transmits its attracting power to all persons who successively come into contact with it, and who are thereby rendered equally magnetic, each as his turn comes.[10] The city tragedians eventually achieve precisely such an extraordinary magnetic impact on the spectators of the Mousetrap: the emotions enacted on stage make the guilty Claudius mad with »choler« (3.2.295), appal those, like Ophelia, who are free of guilt; and confound ignoramuses like Polonius. The success of the Mousetrap disproves Hamlet's assumption that, in order to exercise such an influence on their audience, the players would need the real »motive and the cue for passion / That I [Hamlet] have.« Hamlet's decision to entrust them with the play likewise shows that he does hope for some form of authentic passion that the players can as it were organically »beget« (3.2.7) on stage and transmit to the audience. It seems that Hamlet gets entangled in his mix of Platonic and Aristotelian leanings. Perhaps he imagines that his collaborative hand in the Mousetrap results in a felicitous compounding of his genuine motive for feeling extreme passion with the players' artful capacity for feigning it. Yet Hamlet's own experience with acting the part of an unhinged young man has taught him that having a real motive does not in itself guarantee the success of the performance. Hamlet's antics have not advanced his revenge as much as the players' Mousetrap does. In spite of lacking a cause, the players' pathos paradoxically seems to possess the required authenticity and to achieve the desired impact: theirs may well be a pathos »for nothing« but it is in itself by no means a nothing.

Hamlet's uneven, opportunistic approach to drama is most evident in the aftermath of the Mousetrap. Whereas during the play he was rather sceptical about its quality, after Claudius' crazed reaction Hamlet has only praise for the Mousetrap. In a rare mood of elation, Hamlet claims all the credit for the play, from which he previously distanced himself through biting criticisms:

> HAMLET. Would not this [the Mousetrap], sir, and a forest of feathers – if the rest of my fortunes turn Turk with me — with two Provincial roses on my razed shoes, get me a fellowship in a cry of players, sir?
> HORATIO. Half a share.
> HAMLET. A whole one, I. (3.2.269-274)

Coupled with his announcement of an alternative career path in theatre (should his royal fortunes fail him), Hamlet's exaggerated pride can pass as a joke. His coup pleases him so much that Hamlet now readily identifies with the theatrical profession in all its garish glory, including its feather and shoe-rose paraphernalia – the sort of vulgar actorly things that he previously scorned. Far from a joke, however, is the symbolic empowerment that the Mousetrap provides the

10 Ibid., 533d-e; 535e-536b

prince with in his plot against the king. Claudius' status has sunken drastically after the representation of kingship on stage in most unbefitting circumstances, amidst the grimaces and cries of popular players. Since Claudius has vicariously participated in theatre's unserious »forest of feathers«, he unsurprisingly becomes a creature of feathers himself: »a very, very – pajock« in Hamlet's hilarious gibe (3.2.278).[11] An anecdote from Elizabeth's later years, which has an uncanny resemblance to the Mousetrap, proves the power of courtly drama to offend and diminish the glory of the sovereign: as a result of a »scandalous representation« before the queen, she »was so angry that she at once entered her chamber using strong language, and the men who held the torches ... left [the actors] in the dark.«[12] In Hamlet's eyes, the theatrical treatment of the king makes him a lesser being: more contemptible and also more assailable. We witness the emboldening effect of the Mousetrap on Hamlet in the prayer scene that follows, in which the prince comes very close to slaying the king. Yet for all the service that drama has rendered to Hamlet, and for all his celebration of the Mousetrap success, the prince does not use drama with respect. In his hands art is a toy and a tool, not an end in itself.

2. The uses of conscience and equity

Hamlet has enlisted the resources of drama in order to »catch the conscience of the King« (2.2.601) and to search it, which constitutes an intrusive and illegitimate exercise even in the face of Claudius' criminality. In accordance with a tradition of moral-legal thinking originally established within medieval canon law, consciences were regarded as sacrosanct territory.[13] Definite restrictions were therefore in place as to who was allowed to »catch« them so as to make them yield, in spite of themselves, evidentiary content. Before the Reformation, it was the clergy who performed this task by the commission and in imitation of the heavenly Judge, the sole authority with full and irresistible access to the depths of the human soul. Claudius in his botched prayer acknowledges this much: before God, he says, we feel »ourselves compell'd / Even to the teeth and forehead of our faults / To give in evidence« (3.3.62-64). But here on earth, in Tudor times, consciences were searched for evidence only at the highest levels

11 I rely on an accepted reading of »pajock« as peacock, but for other variant readings see Jenkins (as note 1), p. 510.

12 Calendar of State Papers, Spanish, 1558 – 1567, p. 375, qtd. in Jenkins (as note 1), p. 304.

13 In my account of the English equity jurisdiction and the genealogy of the concepts of equity and conscience, I follow among others John Hamilton Baker, *The Oxford History of the Laws of England: 1483 – 1558*, Oxford 2003, especially pp. 39-48 and 171-209.

of the legal system, by the Court of Chancery and the Star Chamber. In contriving to wring another man's inviolable conscience, Hamlet as it were invests himself with a power equal at least to that of the Lord Chancellor and the Privy Council. But who was the Lord Chancellor, and in whose authority was his ultimately grounded? Under Elizabeth, Chancery prided itself on being the exclusive transmitter of the »conscience of the Queen« and Sir Christopher Hatton, Elizabeth's favourite chancellor, was the first official who graced his person with that title.[14] Frank Kermode has good reasons to hear a pun in Hamlet's resolution to »catch the conscience of the King«, which can also be read as ›to catch the King's chief councillor‹ and thereby, in a roundabout way, the king himself.[15] To be sure, the Mousetrap closes with a moral force upon Claudius and also with a mortal force upon Polonius, his councillor, who is killed in the uproar caused by the play while being mistaken for the king – a mistake that makes sense in the context of Elizabethan ideas about how monarchical authority passes into the Lord Chancellor and transforms him into a royal stand-in. The relation of surrogacy between king and councillor is suggested in Hamlet's comment on murdering Polonius: »A bloody deed! almost as bad, good mother, / As kill a king« (3.4.27-28). It has also been anticipated in the anecdote that Polonius volunteers about how in his student years he was cast as Julius Caesar and assassinated in a university play (3.2.102).

The puns and twists that impinge on Hamlet's scheme are symptomatic of its overall ironic character: while acting against the king in the name of justice, Hamlet invokes a legal ideology of conscience grounded in the monarch's supremacy and in his ability to delegate his supreme power to his officials. As Lowell Gallagher comments

> the discourse of conscience inhabited the Tudor discourse of power in its most exalted form, imparting a rhetoric of inviolability to the monarch that exemplified both the prerogative, in the regnum, of the *princeps* – whose conscience contained the *arcana imperii*, the secrets of state – and, in the *sacerdotium*, the prerogative described by Paul, and appropriated by pontiffs and anointed princes alike, of the »spiritual man«, who »judges all, but himself is judged by none« (1 Cor. 2:15).[16]

The deeper we look into Elizabethan jurisprudence, the more it can reveal about Hamlet's legal pun on »the conscience of the King« and about his audacity to

14 Noted by Samuel E. Thorne, »Preface«, in: Edward Hake, *Epieikeia. A Dialogue on Equity in Three Parts*, ed. D. E. C. Yale, London 1953, p.viii.

15 Frank Kermode, *Shakespeare, Spenser, Donne: Renaissance Essays*, New York 1971, p. 53.

16 Lowell Gallagher, *Medusa's Gaze: Casuistry and Conscience in the Renaissance*, Stanford, Calif., 1991, pp. 9-10.

become, in emulation of the monarch, a conscience expert while paving the way for a potential regicide. The proceedings of the royal courts of Chancery and the Star Chamber relied on the interplay between a searched and a searching conscience, belonging to defendant and chancellor respectively. The ultimate searching conscience, immaculate and supreme though earthly, was that of the monarch, who symbolically presided in court at all times through his or her representation in the person of the chancellor. Since to pry into the conscience of another fellow creature was no simple matter, humanity required of the searcher to bring to this task probity, erudition, a philosophical mind cognizant with the universal principles of ethics and politics, and piety in religious matters. In the Elizabethan context the common law, as professional training and practice, certainly produced men of the world who were both intelligent and urbane, yet that by itself rarely qualified them as searchers of consciences.[17] At the highest levels of the legal system in particular, most Lord Chancellors and council members were jurists with a broader background, which included some familiarity with civil law and the closely related ecclesiastical tradition of jurisprudence.[18]

Institutionally, the domain of the conscience experts was known as equity and comprised, among others, the courts of Chancery and the Star Chamber. Equity, or fairness, functioned as a supplement and a corrective of the common law when the common law proved too rigid or, due to its commitment to precedent and standardized writs, could not cover the infinite variety of idiosyncratic cases that real life spawned. Equity was thus a profoundly thoughtful and interpretive principle because, in order to supersede legalistic justice, equity had to be wiser than the law. Most importantly, the judges of equity courts were interested in exploring aspects of a case that the common law could not recognize as hard or relevant evidence. Many such aspects depended on the conscience and the overall moral identity of the defendant, and potentially also on those of the plaintiff. According to Aristotle, for example, equity teaches us »to ask not what a man is now but what he has always or usually been« as well as »not to consider so much the actions of the accused as his intentions, nor this or that detail so much as the whole story.«[19]

Although Hamlet announces the Mousetrap as a trap for a single mouse, the play in reality serves as the court where two consciences deliver their case to be decided by a third one, that of the examiner-arbiter. The searching and interpreting conscience is that of Hamlet, a sophisticated, learned young man, and something of a moralizer. The part of an equity jurist suits Hamlet more

17 On education in the common law Inns, see Jackie Watson's article in this issue.

18 On the continued intellectual influence of canon law even after the Reformation, see D. E. C. Yale, »Introduction«, in: Edward Hake (as note 14), p. xiii.

19 Aristotle, *Rhetoric*, trs. W. Heinemann, Cambridge, MA, 1947, 1374b.

than that of an avenger. Next is the conscience of the king, whose moral nature exhibits a number of flaws even before the Ghost accuses him of murder. In line with Aristotelian equity thinking, Hamlet has begun his evaluation of Claudius' overall character early on, finding him a swinish drunkard and boisterous reveller (1.4.8-10), a lustful man, deficient as a mourner, and too quick in possessing himself of a widow's bed and her dead husband's estate. The common law mind might remain unimpressed with most of these facts about Claudius' personality, yet an equity thinker will take them all into consideration so as to determine how a brother's murder possibly fits into this whole picture. He may also use his knowledge of Claudius as a man of passions and pleasures to decide what strategy of interrogation and conscience reading would yield the best fruits with this particular man. Hamlet is wise enough to do precisely this. Since Claudius is a man of passions and drama a preeminent stirrer of passions, Hamlet's choice of a stratagem naturally gravitates towards the murder tragedy. And since Claudius loves leisure activities in a mindless way and even recommends them as a cure for Hamlet's melancholy (2.2.15; 3.1.27), he is more likely to be caught off guard if the interrogation takes on the appearance of a courtly entertainment given by Hamlet. But while Claudius can be interrogated, be it even in a covert way, this is not the case with the Ghost, whose conscience is the third, indirect participant in the Mousetrap court affair in the part of a plaintiff. Since the Ghost initiated the action against Claudius in the first place, Hamlet must come to a conclusion about the ghost's moral and existential nature: about whether he is »an honest ghost« (1.5.144) with divinely approved intentions or an impersonating »damned ghost« (3.2.82) with bad designs upon Hamlet and Denmark.

While it is problematic enough that Hamlet, a mortal, should put on trial (albeit indirectly) the veracity of a spiritual creature such as the Ghost, whose business with Hamlet may have God's approval, it is still more unsettling to the early modern sensibility that Hamlet should pry into the secrets of the king's conscience. The unsearchability of the sovereign's interiority is decreed multiple times in the Book of Proverbs: »The heaven for height, and the earth for depth, and the heart of kings is unsearchable«.[20] The same idea was invoked throughout the Tudor and Stuart eras, and Bacon, one of James' chancellors, was among the intellectuals who embraced it wholeheartedly as »that effect which the Scripture speaketh of, that the ›king's heart is inscrutable‹« in part due to the plethora of »representations of perils and shadows« accumulated in it.[21] Many of these perils, as Bacon explains, derive from the king's domestic affairs and his relationship

20 »Book of Proverbs«, 25:3: *The Bible. Authorized King James Version with Apocrypha*, ed. Robert Carroll and Stephen Prickett, Oxford 2008.

21 Francis Bacon, »Of Empire«, in: *Essays*, in: *The Major Works*, ed. Brian Vickers, Oxford 2002, p. 376.

to his courtiers, family members, and subjects, who constantly try to interpret and guess the king's inmost thoughts and intentions.[22]

To counteract presumptuous attempts at getting too close to the king in thought or action, the courtly advice of the Book of Proverbs enjoins subordinates to keep their distance from the king's person in a manner that suggests not just self-effacement but almost, if need be, self-sacrifice: »When thou sittest to eat with a ruler, consider diligently what is before thee; And put a knife to thy throat, if thou be a man given to appetite. Be not desirous of his dainties, for they are deceitful meat«.[23] Although there is no banquet scene proper in *Hamlet*, the Mousetrap gathers the characters in the way that banquets do in other tragedies. As Hamlet is welcoming Claudius to the Mousetrap, he broaches the figurative subject of who eats what at Elsinore. But instead of offering to slash his own gullet before he encroaches on kings' dainties, as Proverbs advises, Hamlet has the audacity to criticize what is dished out to him at the royal table in a tone of sarcastic praise: »Excellent, i'faith, of the chameleon's dish. I eat the air, promise-crammed« (3.2.93). The nothingness of air, which may satiate the chameleon but which leaves Hamlet starving, illustrates well the import of Proverbs' »deceitful meat«. In addition, the likely pun on air/heir sounds a threatening note and allows us to imagine a cannibalization of the heir, at the expense of either heir Hamlet or heir Claudius, to whom the crown of Denmark has passed from his brother only too recently.[24] Hamlet concludes his criticism of Claudius' ›kitchen of state‹ by commenting that »you cannot feed capons« with »promise-crammed« air. The image of the capon, a castrated cock fattened for slaughter, once again unites the two disturbing ideas of being given to eat and being eaten. Insofar as the ›kitchen of state‹ is the kitchen of the king's conscience, where the concocted secrets and dark recipes of government are brewing, Hamlet's culinary comments represent yet another of his essays as a conscience searcher and wringer. Characteristically, Claudius tries to disavow Hamlet's teases in both their silly literal meaning and their dismaying allusions, which by now Claudius is in a position to guess rightly: »I have nothing with this answer, Hamlet. These words are not mine« (3.2.95-96).

While Claudius just means to communicate that he does not accept Hamlet's words as relevant to him, the defensiveness of his rejoinder darkly prefigures Claudius' predicament during the play that, under Hamlet's direction, will put into Claudius' mouth an actor's words and pretend that they are his. As discussed earlier, the word »rank« from the speech that Hamlet has penned for the part of Lucianus indeed becomes a word of self-accusation that Claudius himself uses

22 Ibid., pp. 377-378.
23 »Book of Proverbs« (as note 20), 23:1-3.
24 Jenkins (as note 1), p. 293.

in the prayer scene. In anticipation of such incriminating parts and speeches as the Mousetrap will impose on him, »these words are not mine« already marks Claudius as a helpless defendant in whose experience conscience searching feels rather like additional conscience loading. Since the Mousetrap is a covert interrogation of Claudius, it suffers from the same infelicities that affected interrogative trials, the usual procedure in equity courts. Although on principle equity was supposed to result in more merciful interpretations of an offense, since it took the measure of how the defendant himself viewed his situation and his acts, in practice equity often imputed more blame than there was to begin with. This compounding of guilt was a side effect of too much examination and too much prying, or what Andrew Zurcher has called an »invasive epistemology.«[25] Especially in a medium as over-clever as the Mousetrap, interrogation can animate the imaginations of both the searcher and the searched until they produce a tale of a crime whose enormity has in the process been augmented. This pattern of development is enabled by the very idea of what conscience is and how it can be used. The Latin *conscientia* literally means ›knowledge with someone‹, that is, »knowledge about another person, which can be used in witness for or against that person.«[26] Conscience is thus a potential traitor that the accused harbours within him: it only awaits the approach of the searching judicial conscience to spill out filthy contents, which often amount to more that the accused has thought he has.

The paradoxes and vagaries of conscience searching bring us full circle back to the problem of Hamlet's use of a theatrical artefact to collect evidence on the case of his father's murder. Conscience searching implicates in its interpretive work two agents, both of whom bear responsibility for how the examination will proceed. The searcher – judge, juror, or chancellor – must realize that he »puts his own conscience on the line« no less than the defendant does.[27] He interrogates, interprets, and arbitrates *in personam* rather than via the impersonal principle of the common law and submits his authority, learning, and moral reason to the fickleness of the case.[28] What conscience is in equitable judgment, that, too, is emotional involvement in theatre, which means that one cannot opt out of it. And while Hamlet worries that he falls short of passion when compared to an actor performing in a tragedy (2.2.554-566), it is odd that he does not reflect on his lack of intense passion as a spectator. As he listens to the Trojan speech, Hamlet gives enough signals that he approves of it, yet he shows no outward

25 Andrew Zurcher, *Shakespeare and Law*, London 2010, p. 234.

26 W. D. Davies, qtd. in Timothy C. Potts, *Conscience in Medieval Philosophy*, Cambridge 1980. p. 2.

27 Zurcher (as note 25), p. 218.

28 On the significance of equity's embodiment *in personam*, see Baker (as note 13), p. 42.

passion despite the moving scene of a father's brutal murder. We should think that as a bereaved spectator of the Trojan scene Hamlet must uncontrollably weep, based on his conviction that he would do so if he were a bereaved actor performing this. As unresponsive audience, Hamlet disproves his own theory of the predictability and inevitability of audience emotion (2.2.558-560; 2.2.584-590), particularly in cases when the dramatic content appears to resemble real-life situations that audience members have experienced. Hamlet is so confident that, if guilty, Claudius must have a strong reaction that he overlooks the fact of his own absent reaction – absent despite the emotional appeal and the potential for identification that the Trojan scene offers him. From beginning to end, Hamlet's understanding of theatre and of the principles of conscience has been too mechanistic. Like Hamlet, theatre and conscience become contaminated by the murder they are enlisted to investigate. Neither art nor equitable justice can be what they are when they fall into the hands of an avenger who bends their codes to his own ends.

Abstracts

Janette Dillon

Spectatorship at the Early Modern English Court [Zuschauen am frühneuzeitlichen englischen Hof]

Der Artikel definiert zentrale Kategorien für die Analyse frühneuzeitlichen Zuschauens. Ausgehend von den Befunden des Kunsthistorikers Jonathan Crary wird deutlich, dass Zuschauen nicht nur Sehen bedeutet, sondern im Kern vor allem, sich einem System von Konventionen und Beschränkungen zu fügen. Quelle der hier vorgestellten Überlegungen bilden die Aufzeichnungen des deutschen Adeligen Lupold von Wedel, der 1584 den Feierlichkeiten zum Jahrestag von Elisabeths Thronbesteigung in London beiwohnte. Der Reisende bemerkte dabei scharfsinnig, dass es nicht so sehr Ziel des an jenem Tag abgehaltenen Turniers war, den ausgelobten Preis zu gewinnen, sondern vielmehr die Königin und die anderen Zuschauer zu amüsieren und zu beeindrucken. Die genaue Untersuchung der Quelle stellt die Wichtigkeit von drei Aspekten des Zuschauens heraus: den Raum, die Zusammensetzung der Zuschauer sowie Zweck und Qualität des Spektakels (wo? wer? wie und warum?). Wenngleich Elisabeth stets zentrale Zuschauerin und zentrale Darstellerin war, so konnten sich Blickregime und Raumordnungen bei verschiedenen Anlässen stark unterscheiden. Der Artikel untersucht hier die königliche Prozession und das Turnier als zwei gegensätzliche Formen des Spektakels, die unterschiedliche Arten des Sehens erforderten und mit unterschiedlichen Arten von Furcht und Freude aufgeladen waren.

Sasha Garwood

Watching Elizabeth Eating. Power and Politics of Penetration [Elisabeth beim Essen zuschauen. Macht und Politik der Penetration]

Essen war am elisabethanischen Hof mit symbolischer Bedeutung befrachtet. Als Herrscherin nutzte Elisabeth aufwendige Feierlichkeiten und seltene Momente geteilten oder gemeinschaftlichen Essens als politische Mittel, die echte oder scheinbare Nähe und Verbundenheit andeuteten. Sowohl Verzehr als auch Verweigerung von Speisen stellten öffentliche Handlungen dar und wurden zum Gegenstand wilder Spekulationen. Veränderungen von Elisabeths Essgewohnheiten und des königlichen Körpers wurden auch von Personen, die gewöhnlich keinen Zugang zur Königin hatten, eifrig diskutiert, ins Ausland übermittelt und genauestens analysiert, um Rückschlüsse auf ihre Absichten, Gefühle, Reaktionen oder mögliche politische Strategien zu ziehen. So wurde der Befund, die Königin sei während der durch Katherine Greys Schwangerschaft ausgelösten Krise »schwindend ... extrem dünn und von der Farbe einer Leiche« gewesen, dem spanischen Gesandten de la Quadra aus »drei verschiedenen Quellen« und von »einer Person, die die Gelegenheit hatte Augenzeuge zu sein« hinterbracht. Tatsächliche oder vermutete Veränderungen in der Nahrungsaufnahme wurden also von höfischen Beobachtern als politisch bedeutsame emotionale Äußerung interpretiert. Der Artikel untersucht Elisabeths sorgfältige und bewusste Verwendung der performativen Sprache von Essen, Hungern und Körperlichkeit und analysiert deren kulturelle Implikationen.

Galena Hashhozheva

The Mousetrap. A Court Spectacle and Its Jurisdiction [Die Mausefalle. Ein höfisches Spektakel und seine Gerichtsbarkeit]

Nach der Aufführung der ›Mausefalle‹ insistiert Polonius, dass Hamlet »zu wilde Streiche macht / Um sie zu dulden«. Streich wird normalerweise als hinterlistige Handlung umschrieben. Doch auch die Bedeutung im Sinne einer Posse – eines Tricks, der belustigt, indem er andere zum Narren hält – ist relevant angesichts des (wenngleich makabren) Vergnügens, das Hamlet aus seinem Stück bezieht. ›Die Mausefalle‹ kann sehr ergiebig im Lichte von Castigliones Theorie des Streichs (ital. burla) gelesen werden. Castiglione beschreibt Späße und Streiche als unverzichtbare Bestandteile des Hoflebens; zum einen weil sie Unterhaltung bieten, zum anderen aber auch weil sie eine moralisch korrektive Funktion haben, wenn der Täter / die Täterin den Charakter seines / ihres Opfers kennt. Streiche bringen die Zielperson dazu, öffentlich ihre moralischen Schwächen und Fehler vorzuführen und können so einen therapeutischen Effekt haben. Der Artikel zeigt, dass ›Die Mausefalle‹ sowohl Castigliones Definition erfüllt als auch von ihr abweicht. Obwohl Hamlet sonst höfische Verhaltensweisen verachtet, macht er sich mit der ›Mausefalle‹ die Gepflogenheiten des höfischen Streichs ganz pragmatisch zunutze. Er gestaltet das moralisch korrektive Muster mit künstlerischem Empfindungsvermögen, seiner epistemologischen Besessenheit und einer kalten Grausamkeit, die es zu einem Wendepunkt seines Handelns machen.

Susanne Scholz

»Dauncings true nobilitie«: Absent Queens in John Davies' Orchestra *and Edmund Spenser's* The Faerie Queene *Book VI. [Abwesende Königinnen in John Davies'* Orchestra *and Edmund Spenser's* The Faerie Queene *Book VI.]*

Der Beitrag untersucht Praktiken und Politiken des königlichen Tanzes. Besonders Elizabeths Tänze mit dem Earl of Leicester haben einen festen Platz im kulturellen Imaginären unserer Zeit; dabei sind historische Quellen über die tanzende Königin äußerst selten. Dichterische Repräsentationen aus den 1590er Jahren, etwa John Davies' *Orchestra* und Buch VI von Spensers *The Faerie Queene* thematisieren hingegen gerade die Weigerung der dargestellten Königinnen, am höfischen Tanz teilzunehmen. Der Artikel untersucht diese poetischen Repräsentationen im Licht einiger tanzhistorischen Neuerungen der Frühen Neuzeit, etwa der neuen Dominanz des Paartanzes, und kommt zu dem Schluss, dass die damit einhergehende (blickgeleitete) Erotisierung der tanzenden Körper es Elisabeth zunehmend unmöglich macht, den *body politic* auf diese Weise zu artikulieren.

Simon Smith

»Flourish. Enter the King sicke«: Exploring Kingship through Musical Spectacle in Richard III *[Untersuchungen zum Königtum anhand des musikalischen Spektakels in* Richard III*]*

Der Artikel widmet sich der einzig aus Trompeten und Trommeln bestehenden Musik in *Richard III*, die, verglichen mit Musik und Liedern in anderen elisabethanischen Dramen, nur selten akademische Aufmerksamkeit bekommt. Die letzten vier Akte des Stücks enthalten jeweils einen Auftritt eines der vier dargestellten Könige (Edward IV., Edward V., Richard II. und Henry VII.), die jeweils mit Trompeten angekündigt werden. Hier wird genauer beleuchtet, welche Instrumente bei solchen Gelegenheiten im Theater Verwendung fanden und welche Konventionen die Erwartungen des Publikums bei ihrem Klang strukturierten. Für zeitgenössische Zuschauer hatten Trommeln und Trompeten klare Bedeutungen, die oft von großer Wichtigkeit für das dramatische Erzählen waren. So verwandelte der Klang von Trompeten das Theater in einen imaginären höfischen Raum, den eine königliche Figur betrat. Aber statt einen eindeutigen, strahlenden Anblick zu bieten, an dem sich die Zuschauer erfreuen könnten, laufen die Auftritte der vier Könige in *Richard III* solchen Erwartungen direkt zuwider und lenken die Aufmerksamkeit so auf die Frage, wie gutes und legitimes Königtum aussehen sollte. Der Artikel zeigt so auf, dass die erfolgreiche dramatische Verwendung von Musik nicht unbedingt großer Mittel und ausgefeilter Instrumentierung bedurfte.

Jackie Watson

»He writes, he railes, he jests, he courts, what not, / And all from out his huge long scraped stock / Of well penn'd playes«: Learning the Performance of Courtiership at the Early Modern Inns of Court. [Das Erlernen der Kunst höfischen Verhaltens an den frühneuzeitlichen Inns of Court]

Die Inns of Court waren in der Frühen Neuzeit gleichermaßen Ausbildungsstätte für Juristen und junge Gentlemen. Viele Studenten hatten nicht nur eine Laufbahn im Rechtswesen, sondern vor allem am königlichen Hof im Auge. Der Aufstieg eines humanistischen Bildungskanons an den Inns of Court und den Universitäten des sechzehnten Jahrhunderts ermöglichte auch nicht-adeligen Studenten, eine Laufbahn im Staatsdienst einzuschlagen. Der Artikel untersucht, wie die breitgefächerte kulturelle Bildung an den Inns of Court junge Männer auf erfolgreiches Auftreten bei Hofe vorbereitete. Zunächst wird dazu die Teilnahme an Festen beleuchtet, welche höfische Hierarchie und Protokoll nachahmten und so diesen Vorbereitungscharakter sichtbar machen. Sodann werden satirische und dramatische Darstellungen des Hofs betrachtet, die mit dem spätelisabethanischen Middle Temple in Verbindung gebracht werden können. Dabei wird die einflussreiche Sicht einer berüchtigten Gruppe junger Autoren auf höfisches Verhalten und höfischen Schein am Ende von Elizabeths Regierungszeit herausgearbeitet.

Notes on Contributors

Janette Dillon is Professor of Drama at the University of Nottingham and works on early English drama. Her most recent publications are *Shakespeare and the Staging of English History* (Oxford University Press, 2012) and *The Language of Space in Court Performance 1400 – 1625* (CUP, 2010).
Earlier books include: *The Cambridge Introduction to Shakespeare's Tragedies* (Cambridge University Press, 2007), *The Cambridge Introduction to Early English Theatre* (Cambridge University Press, 2006), *Performance and Spectacle in Hall's Chronicle* (London: Society for Theatre Research, 2002), and *Theatre, Court and City 1595 – 1610: Drama and Social Space in London* (Cambridge University Press, 2000). She has published numerous articles on early English drama and performance, and has recently been working on articles on the history of the discovery-space and scenic memory; she is co-editing a special edition (on space) of *Journal of Medieval and Early Modern Studies.*

Daniel Dornhofer is a Lecturer in British Literature and Culture at the University of Frankfurt am Main. His main research interests are in the field of early modern studies (Petrarchism, Jacobean court culture in Scotland and England, political language) and Anglo-Jewish literature and culture. His latest publication was *Petrarkistischer Diskurs und höfische Kommunikation im Wandel: Strategien schottischer Dichter, 1580 – 1625*. Heidelberg: Winter 2012. He is currently working on his research project »The Jewish Face – Typology in Anglo-Jewish Literature, Race Science and Zionism, 1890 – 1930«.

Sasha Garwood is a PhD Candidate at University College London. Her thesis is entitled ›*The skull beneath the skin*‹: *elite women and self-starvation in early modern England.* She holds prior degrees from Keble College, Oxford and University College, London. She has published articles and reviews on food, sex and the female body in early modern drama.

Galena Hashhozheva (B. A. Sofia University and University of Cologne 2001; PhD Harvard University 2009) holds a postdoctoral fellowship and teaches Renaissance literature in the English Department at Ludwig-Maximilians-Universität, Munich. Before coming to Munich, she served as a College Fellow and Lecturer in Renaissance literature at Harvard. While still a doctoral candidate, she was awarded the Harvard Presidential Scholarship for her dissertation »The System of the Intellectual Virtues in Edmund Spenser's *Faerie Queene.*« She is currently working on a book project titled »Unsettling the Renaissance: Nomads, Hordes, and Brigands from Marlowe's Tamburlaine to Milton's Satan.« She has published or has articles forthcoming on Spenser and Shakespeare.

Susanne Scholz is Professor of English Literature and Culture at the University of Frankfurt am Main. She has held teaching posts at the Universities of Frankfurt, Siegen and Paderborn. Her main research interests and publications are in the field of early modern, eighteenth- and nineteenth-century English literature, gender studies, medical humanities and visual culture studies. She is currently working on a project on visual practices at the court of Elizabeth I. Her major book publications are: *Body Narratives: Writing the Nation and Fashioning the Subject in Early Modern England.* London: Macmillan 2000, *Objekte und Erzählungen. Subjektivität und kultureller Dinggebrauch im England des frühen 18. Jahrhunderts.* Königstein: Helmer 2004, and *Phantasmatic Knowledge. Visions of the Human and the Scientific Gaze in English Literature, 1880 – 1930.* Heidelberg: Winter (forthcoming).

Simon Smith is a PhD Candidate at Birkbeck, University of London, supported by the AHRC. He is a Research Associate (Music) at Shakespeare's Globe, assisting with the reconstruction of a Jacobean indoor theatre that will open in January 2014. He teaches at both Birkbeck and Shakespeare's Globe. He is editing *The Senses in Early Modern England, 1558 – 1660* with Jackie Watson, Amy Kenny and S. J. Wiseman (Manchester University Press, Forthcoming), and will contribute a chapter on »*Antony and Cleopatra* and visual musical experience« to this collection. He regularly provides music research (and occasionally gives musical direction) to productions of plays by Shakespeare and his contemporaries. His research interests include music in early modern drama, Jacobean performance practice, theatre history, and sensory studies.

Jackie Watson is a PhD student at Birkbeck, London, after an MA there and an undergraduate degree from Somerville College, Oxford. Under the supervision of Professor Susan Wiseman, her thesis takes Sir Thomas Overbury as a case study to examine the changing representation of courtiership and ambition on the early modern stage. A Graduate Teaching Assistant at Birkbeck, she reviews for the *TLS* and has delivered papers to recent conferences in London, St Andrews and Stratford-upon-Avon. She is co-editing *The Senses in Early Modern England, 1558 – 1600* with Simon Smith, Amy Kenny and Sue Wiseman, and organized an international conference in February this year at Middle Temple Hall, on Renaissance Men in the Middle Temple. Her research interests are the early modern Inns of Court, playgoing audiences, courtly appearance and verbal deception.

Aus *Zeitsprünge* 1 (1997), Heft 1:
Alessandro Nova, »Konservative Theorie und innovative Praxis bei den Franziskaner-Observanten als Auftraggeber der bildenden Künste«
Herrmann Schrödter, »Diskurs statt Gewalt. Nikolaus von Kues und Thomas More auf dem Weg zur Religionsphilosophie«
Heide Wunder, Helga Zöttlein, Barbara Hoffmann, »Konfession, Religiosität und politisches Handeln von Frauen vom ausgehenden 16. bis zum Beginn des 18. Jahrhunderts«
Martin Windisch, »›When there is no visible power to keep in awe‹. Staatstheorie und Bildform bei Thomas Hobbes«
Bertram Schefold, »Nicolaus Oresmius. Die Geldlehre des Spätmittelalters«

Aus *Zeitsprünge* 1 (1997), Heft 2:
Jean-Claude Schmitt, »Plädoyer für eine komparative Geschichte der religiösen Bilder«
Klaus Reichert, »›Ich bin ich.‹ Auftritte neuer Formen des Bösen in der Frühen Neuzeit«
Victoria von Flemming, »Die böse Schöne. Eine Weiblichkeitskonstruktion in der Literatur und bildenden Kunst der Frühneuzeit Italiens«
Simon Huber, Christian Schmitt, Bettina Mathes, »Nation und Nationalismus: Modelle – Geschichte – Probleme«
Christian Schmitt, »Writing the Nation in Early Modern England: The Case of Rhetoric and Poetics«
Karin Wilhelm, »Locating the Individual. Filarete's *Treatise on Architecture* 1464«

Zeitsprünge 1 (1997), Heft 3/4:
»Aspekte der Gegenreformation«, hrsg. v. Victoria von Flemming

Aus *Zeitsprünge* 2 (1998), Heft 1/2:
Stephen Greenblatt, »Hamlet im Fegefeuer«
Alexander Perrig, »Leonardo: Die Rekonstruktion menschlicher Bewegung«
Wolfgang Neuber, »Die Mauern, die Wendeltreppe, der Dom und der Überblick«
Eckhard Lobsien, »Wahrnehmung in Miltons *Paradise Lost*«
Christos Baloglou, »Georgios Gemistos-Plethon und Sphairos von Borysthenes«

Zeitsprünge 2 (1998), Heft 3/4:
»Kaspar Schoppe (1576 – 1649). Philologe im Dienste der Gegenreformation«, hrsg. von Herbert Jaumann

Zeitsprünge 3 (1999), Heft 1/2:
Sonderheft zu Giordano Bruno.
Mit Beiträgen von Stephen Clucas, Jean Seidengart, Wolfgang Neuser, Klaus Reichert, Wilhelm Schmidt-Biggemann, Klaus-Jürgen Grün, Alfred Schmidt, Enno Rudolph, Paul Richard Blum, Wolfgang Wildgen, Leen Spruit, Walter G. Saltzer, Karl-Otto Apel.

Aus *Zeitsprünge* 3 (1999), Heft 3/4:
Norman Cohn, »Wie die Zeit ihre Erfüllung fand«
Peter Schäfer, »Armageddon: Endzeitphantasien in Judentum, Christentum und Islam«
Bernard McGinn, »Apocalypticism and Mysticism. Aspects of the History of Their Interaction«
Michael Milway, »Apocalyptic Reform and Forerunners of the End. Berthold Pürstinger, Bishop of Chiemsee († 1543)«
Richard Popkin, »Der Millenarismus des siebzehnten Jahrhunderts«
Martina Mittag, »Re-Gendering Utopia: The Vitalist Universe of Margaret Cavendish«
David S. Katz, »Messianic Revolution«
Dominic Pettmann, »After the Orgy: Millennial Panic and the Virtual Apocalypse«
Jan Wagner, »Apocalypse How? Endzeitphantasien im populären Film«
Ulrich Konrad, »Apocalypsis cum figuris musices. Musikalische Annäherungen an die Offenbarung des Johannes«

Aus *Zeitsprünge* 4 (2000), Heft 1/2:
Frank Kermode, »Millenium und Apokalypse«
Patricia Crone, »Islam and Messianic Politics«
Mark R. Bell, »The Millenarianism of Robert Maton (1607 – 1653?)«
Raz Chen, Kepler's Optics: The Mistaken Identity of a Baroque Spectator«
Richard Cole, »Spreading Reformation Ideas: The Work and Medical Writing of Dr. Burchard Mithob in Sixteenth-Century Calenberg«
Rémy Roussetzki, »When Eve Answers Back: the Impossible of Paradise Lost
Sibylla Flügge, »Gleiche Rechte für Frauen und Männer: greifbar nah – unendlich fern. Traditionslinien vom Mittelalter bis zur Aufklärung«
Barbara Stollberg-Rilinger, »Was heißt landständische Repräsentation? Überlegungen zur argumentativen Verwendung eines politischen Begriffs«

Aus *Zeitsprünge* 4 (2000), Heft 3:
Manfred Vasold, »Die Aufnahme der Gregorianischen Kalenderreform im Fränkischen Kreis«
Ralf Haekel, »Zum Verhältnis von Theaterpraxis und Drama in der Frühen Neuzeit. Heinrich Julius' *Susanna* und die Englischen Komödianten«
Dietmar Till, »*Affirmation und Subversion.* Zum Verhältnis von ›platonischen‹ und ›rhetorischen‹ Elementen in der frühneuzeitlichen Poetik«
Stephan Kraft, »Höfischer Barockroman und gelehrter Traktat. Gratwanderungen zwischen honnêteté und Pedanterie«
Rémy Roussetzki, »Visual Grotesque and Denial of Castration in Rabelais«
Frank Linhard, »Keplers Schrift über den hexagonalen Schnee. Eine Einführung«
Johannes Kepler, »Über den hexagonalen Schnee«

Zeitsprünge 4 (2000), Heft 4:
»Jedem das Seine. Abgrenzungen und Grenzüberschreitungen im Leipzig des 17. und 18. Jahrhunderts«, hrsg. v. Heide Wunder

Zeitsprünge 5 (2001), Heft 1/2:
Peter Sillem: »Saturns Spuren. Aspekte des Wechselspiels von Melancholie und Volkskultur in der Frühen Neuzeit«

Aus *Zeitsprünge* 5 (2001), Heft 3/4:
Romano Nanni, »Galileo Galilei 1613 – 1616: Naturphilosophie und Bibelexegese«
Mathias Pozsgai, »Unmittelbare Vermittlung: Anatomie und Autorschaft in *De humani corporis fabrica* (1543)«
Jamey Hecht, »Tragedy, Hamlet and Luther«
Albert Schirrmeister, »Traum und Wissen in der Frühen Neuzeit: Erste Annäherungen«
Thomas O. Beebee, »They Built Millenium: Jesuits und Guaranís 1610 –1768«
Wolfgang Detel, Claus Zittel, »Hobbes und die Historiographie«

Zeitsprünge 6 (2002), Heft 1-4:
»Das Geheimnis am Beginn der europäischen Moderne«, hrsg. v. Gisela Engel, Brita Rang, Klaus Reichert und Heide Wunder in Zusammenarbeit mit Jonathan Elukin

Aus *Zeitsprünge* 7 (2003), Heft 1:
Volker Reinhardt, »Rom im Zeitalter der Konfessionalisierung. Kritische Überlegungen zu einem Epochendeutungskonzept«

Jürgen Klein, »Bacon's Quarrel with the Aristotelians«
Franz Strunz, »Walter Charleton, Epikur und die Liebe«
Ralf Haekel, »›For there is nothing either good or bad but thinking makes it so‹. Zu Walter Benjamins Hamletinterpretation«
Frank Linhard, »Atomismuskritik. Ununterscheidbarkeit und Prinzipienphysik bei Leibniz anhand eines Fragments aus den nachgelassenen philosophischen Schriften«

Zeitsprünge 7 (2003), Heft 2/3:
»Berichten, Erzählen, Beherrschen. Wahrnehmung und Repräsentation in der frühen Kolonialgeschichte Europas«, hrsg. v. Susanna Burghartz, Maike Christadler, Dorothea Nolde

Aus *Zeitsprünge* 7 (2003), Heft 4:
Sergius Kodera, »Masculine / Feminine. The concept of matter in Leone Ebreo's *Dialoghi d'amore*«
Ruth Berger, »Von Eigenkontrolle zu Selbstkontrolle. Paradigmenwechsel im jüdischen Diskurs über sexuelle Sünden in der frühen Neuzeit«
Andreas Kraß, »Schwarze Galle, schwarze Kunst. Poetik der Melancholie in der *Historia von D. Johann Fausten*«
Claudia Swan, »Eyes wide shut. Early modern imagination, demonology, and the visual arts«
William N. West, »Atomies and Anatomies. Giulio Camillo, early modern dissection, and the classic poem«
Thomas Ahnert, »›Nullius in verba‹: Autorität und Experiment in der Frühen Neuzeit. Das Beispiel Johann Christoph Sturms (1635 – 1703)«

Zeitsprünge 8 (2004), Heft 1/2:
Christian Schmitt-Kilb: »›Never was the Albion Nation without Poetrie‹. Poetik, Rhetorik und Nation im England der Frühen Neuzeit«

Zeitsprünge 8 (2004), Heft 3/4:
»Technik in der Frühen Neuzeit – Schrittmacher der europäischen Moderne«, hrsg. v. Gisela Engel und Nicole C. Karafyllis

Zeitsprünge 9 (2005), Heft 1/2:
»Zergliederungen – Anatomie und Wahrnehmung in der Frühen Neuzeit«, hrsg. v. Albert Schirrmeister unter Mitarbeit von Mathias Pozsgai

Zeitsprünge 9 (2005), Heft 3/4:
»Kirchen, Märkte und Tavernen. Erfahrungs- und Handlungsräume in der Frühen Neuzeit«, hrsg. v. Renate Dürr und Gerd Schwerhoff

Zeitsprünge 10 (2006), Heft 1/2:
René Descartes: »Les météores / Die Meteore«

Aus *Zeitsprünge* 10 (2006), Heft 3/4:
Sabine Lucia Müller: »*Romancing the (unhappy) queen*. Emplotment frühneuzeitlichen weiblichen Königtums am Beispiel Mary Tudors (1553 – 1558)«
Harald Bollbuck: »Wissensorganisation und fromme Handlungsanleitung – die Ordnung der Historien bei David Chytraeus«
Dana Jalobeanu »The Politics of Science and the Origins of Modernity Building consensus in the Early Royal Society«
Jürgen Klein: »Eastward Ho! Hakluyt's Principal Voyages on English 16th century Seafarers to the Baltic and Eastern Europe«
Daniel Damler: »Pars pro toto Die juristische Erfindung der Entdeckung Amerikas«
Christopher Pierce: »Take Four: Another Perspective on Dutch Colonisation in New York«

Zeitsprünge 11 (2007), Heft 1/2:
»Notions of Space and Time. Early Modern Concepts and Fundamental Theories / Begriffe von Raum und Zeit. Frühneuzeitliche Konzepte und fundamentale Theorien«, hrsg. v. Frank Linhard und Peter Eisenhardt

Zeitsprünge 11 (2007), Heft 3/4:
»Nation – Europa – Welt: Identitätsentwürfe vom Mittelalter bis 1800«, hrsg. v. Ingrid Baumgärtner, Claudia Brinker-von der Heyde, Andreas Gardt, Franziska Sick

Zeitsprünge 12 (2008), Heft 1/2:
»Lire Michel de Certeau / Michel de Certeau lesen«, hrsg. v. Philippe Büttgen und Christian Jouhaud

Aus *Zeitsprünge* 12 (2008), Heft 3/4:
Sylvie Taussig: »Introduction à Gabriel Naudé, *Discours* ...«
Gabriel Naudé: »Discours sur les divers incendies du Mont Vésuve, et particulièrement sur le dernier qui commença le 16 décembre 1631«
Claus Zittel: »La terra trema. Unordnung als Thema und Form im frühneuzeitlichen Katastrophengedicht«

Gerd Grübler: »Erkenntnisskepsis, Geschichtspessimismus und die Neue Wissenschaft im England des 17. Jahrhundert«

Aus *Zeitsprünge* 13 (2009), Heft 1/2:
Andreas Mahler: »*Beginning in the middle*. Strategie und Taktik an den Inns of Court«
Thomas Leinkauf: »Leibniz und Platon«
Tobias Winnerling: »›Man hat aber nicht Ursache, auf diese Auctoris Beschreibung von Formosa viel zu bauen‹. Die Insel Formosa in Zedlers Universal-Lexicon und bei George Psalmanazar«
Claus Bernet: »Größe und Erscheinungsort des Himmlischen Jerusalem in der Frühen Neuzeit«
Michael Spang: »Anthropologie und Geschlechterbild in Anna Maria von Schurmans *Dissertatio* über Frauenbildung«
Sabine Blackmore: »Matchless and yet Melancholy? Weibliche Melancholie in den Gedichten von Katherine Philips«

Zeitsprünge 13 (2009), Heft 3/4:
»Konjunkturen der Höflichkeit in der Frühen Neuzeit«, hrsg. v. Gisela Engel, Brita Rang, Susanne Scholz, Johannes Süßmann

Zeitsprünge 14 (2010), Heft 1/2:
»Frankfurt im Schnittpunkt der Diskurse. Strategien und Institutionen literarischer Kommunikation im späten Mittelalter und in der frühen Neuzeit«, hrsg.v. Robert Seidel und Regina Toepfer

Aus *Zeitsprünge* 14 (2010), Heft 3/4:
Ursula Paintner und Barbara Scholz: »Homagius' *De Origine Iesvvitarvm Carmen* – Zwischen Humanismus und Konfessionalisierung«
Philipp Hahn: »Geliebter Nächster oder böser Nachbar? Die Bewertung der Außenwelt in der ›Hausväterliteratur‹«
Willem van Hoorn und Kees Bertels: »Harvey's Unexpected Invention of the Blood Circulation«
Sergius Kondera: »Der Philosoph als Porträtist. Malerei und Antiplatonische Philosophie in Giordano Brunos Komödie *Candelaio* (1582)«
Samuela Marconcini: »The Conversion of Jewish Women in Florence (1599 – 1799)«
Susanne Scholz: »The Queen's Eye and the Queen's Heart. Elizabeth I *en miniature*«

Zeitsprünge 15 (2011), Heft 1:
»Soziale Ungleichheit und ständische Gesellschaft. Theorien und Debatten in der Frühneuzeitforschung«, hrsg. v. Marian Füssel und Thomas Weller

Zeitsprünge 15 (2011), Heft 2/3:
»Gelehrte Polemik. Intellektuelle Konfliktverschärfungen um 1700«, hrsg. v. Kai Bremer und Carlos Spoerhase

Aus *Zeitsprünge* 15 (2011), Heft 4:
Fabian Jonietz: »Die Topik des hässlichen Künstlers. Zum Körperbild als Reflexionsfläche von Diskurs und Kritik«
Julia Weitbrecht: »Die Performanz von Weltleben und Konversion. Maria Magdalena im geistlichen Spiel«
Christina Wald: »›I would eat his heart‹. Liebeshunger und Blutdurst in Shakespeares *Much Ado About Nothing*«
Harald Kleinschmidt: »Normwandel durch Normdiffusion. Reguliertes Körperverhalten in Militär und Tanz vornehmlich des 17. und 18. Jahrhunderts«

Zeitsprünge 16 (2012), Heft 1/2:
»Orientbegegnungen deutscher Protestanten in der Frühen Neuzeit«, hrsg. v. Markus Friedrich und Alexander Schunka

Aus *Zeitsprünge* 16 (2012), Heft 3/4:
Elfi Bettinger: »Bad Timing? Eine missglückte Kaffeehaus-Proklamation von King Charles II im Jahre 1675«
Barbara Orland: »Ernährungsphysiologie à la Descartes«
Helge Wendt: »Interkulturelle Essensgeschichte am Beispiel zweier deutschsprachiger Jesuitenmissionare in Südamerika (18. Jahrhundert)«
Susanne Gruß: »Thomas Middleton's Gothic Nighmares«
Volkhard Wels: »Zwischen Spiritualismus, Hermetik und lutherischer ›Orthodoxie‹: Zu Hans-Georg Kempers Vorsgeschichte der Naturlyrik«
Christa Kenllwolf King: »Prophetic and Political Vision in Shakespeare's *Tempest*: John Dee as a Model for Prospero«
Andreas Kraß: »Der Finger Gottes. Die Spürbarkeit der Zeichen bei Hugo von St. Viktor und Johannes Bissel«
Stefan Schlelein: »Older than Rome? Spanish Historiography in Search of Its Own Antiquity«